AF255658

What the Ancestors Knew

What the Ancestors Knew

Reclaiming Faith in Western Zen Practice

JOANNE P. MILLER

RESOURCE *Publications* · Eugene, Oregon

Resource Publications
An Imprint of Wipf and Stock Publishers
199 W. 8th Ave., Suite 3
Eugene, OR 97401

www.wipfandstock.com

PAPERBACK ISBN: 978-1-6667-8472-5
HARDCOVER ISBN: 978-1-6667-8473-2
EBOOK ISBN: 978-1-6667-8474-9

11/28/23

Whosever unwavering faith is established in the Thus Gone One, whose virtues are praised by the Noble Ones, has faith in the Community and has right view, they are not poor, nor is their life useless.

—Anguttara Nikaya (*The Numerical Discourses*)

One who practices the Buddha Way above all should have faith in the Buddha Way.

—Gakudo Yojinshu (*Points to Watch in Practicing the Way*)

In faith there is nirvana.

—Dasheng Qixin Lun (*The Awakening of Mahayana Faith*)

Contents

1

Faith Met

I MET ZEN FAITH the very moment I walked in the door of the Mountain Moon Zen Society, but it wasn't until I had cancer that I fully realized it. That's when it became clear for the first time that faith was truly an important and useful element of the Zen Way. In the midst of suffering, faith became more than just confidence in the Buddha and his teachings, it became what I now call faith *as* Buddha too.

I met this latter kind of faith one day during chemotherapy when nothing was working for me. I had taken to using Zen prayer beads and reciting *namu myoho renge kyo*, the central mantra chanted within all forms of Nichiren Buddhism. The Saddharmapundarika Sutra (Lotus Sutra) is my favorite sutra and I needed something short and meaningful to recite when I had no energy.

At one point, however, nothing worked. I threw my beads down in disgust. Mindfulness had helped during needles, *koan* practice during MRIs and bead work throughout chemo, but this time absolutely none of my tried-and-true methods came through for me.

For some unknown reason, Zen master Dogen came to mind: "That the ten thousand beings advance and confirm the self is called awakening." When I began to settle down into this, the most amazing actualization of faith happened in the form of *gyoji dokan* or the circle of the Way in continuous practice.

Dogen taught that there is not a moment's gap between aspiration, practice, enlightenment, and nirvana. As I explain in chapter 7, this involves the unity of practice and attainment in the here-and-now; a continuous and full engagement with whatever is going on.

In that moment and many others after that, everything "advanced" so that the Buddha was the chemo and the chemo Buddha. So too was the beeping monitor, the pain and nausea, and the rather pedestrian hospital meals. The gap between the cancer and me fell away, once again confirming that it is not suffering that goes away but the person who suffers. This was faith as Buddha; the goal and the Way as one.

The kind of faith I was most familiar with was trust and confidence in the Way. It meant knowing that Zen actually works, and that suffering is a part of life. Trust in the efficacy of the Dharma is confidence in our own buddha nature because the Dharma and buddha nature are one and the same. In my case, I trusted in the fact that I could have a part of my chest taken off and still be buddha nature itself. Regardless of what happens to me—ultimately there is nothing gained, nothing lost.

The result of this was that dealing with the ego surrounding that was thankfully not a formidable task. I felt no loss in value. So, while this kind of trust wavered from time to time, what I now recognize as faith or the manifestation of confidence in the practice, acted as sustenance for a very sick person. I felt grateful that I had experienced the practice long enough to develop the confidence that Zen would stand me in good stead.

Yet at some point, it also became clear that taking concrete steps *in* faith and trust had a different quality to *being* faith. In other words, taking faith in the Dharma *to deal with* cancer was qualitatively different from *being* the faith-cancer itself. Faith in the practice I had, but completely and fully being it was a whole other thing.

In my Zen tradition, the Sanbo-Zen lineage, koan practice is emphasized. Even though the school has stated that *shikantaza* or silent illumination meditation (one iteration of faith as Buddha) is *Saijojo-Zen* (Supreme Vehicle Zen), the highest form of Zen, in my experience it has not featured much in the koan curriculum. Rather, the practice focuses primarily on faith as trust in inherent buddha nature. Gradually enhancing my awareness through koan work was the way in which I ended up experiencing *kensho*, the confirmation of the true self.

So *shusho itto*, the oneness of practice and enlightenment, does in fact, mature as the practice matures. However, in my experience, it has not been the explicit focus of practice until advanced stages of koan practice. Nonetheless, from early chemo sessions onward, meeting each moment as oneness and as a unified expression of faith and practice greatly enhanced actualization of essential nature in my daily life, one of the stated aims of Sanbo-zen.

It also kindled my interest in the relationship between Zen and faith. I began to inquire about the types of faith we have in Zen, and its many functions or manifestations. What I found only reinforced my own experiential findings—that faith is something we can successfully use but few Western Zen Buddhists know this. I have written this book in the hope that others will profit from a consideration (or reconsideration) of faith and its benefits in Zen practice as well as form a bridge of understanding to faith-based schools such as Pure Land and Nichiren Buddhisms.

2

Faith As It Is Seen In the West

FAITH GETS A BAD rap these days. Unfortunately, much of it deserved. It is easy to dislike faith. 9/11 showed us what happens when faith is used as the justification for religious actions which are violent, unreasonable, and extreme. People have died because of faith. Through its own actions, it often puts itself out there as a straw man easily set on fire. It is no surprise that many of us in the West associate it with uncritical religious belief and rigid dogma.

For some of us, faith is even scarring. In the name of faith, we may have had to endure a childhood of submission to an external authority such as a Church, a faith leader or even members of our own family. Faith can separate us into believers and non-believers with disastrous results. No wonder that we equate it with unfounded beliefs, wishful thinking, a lack of logic and narrow-minded prejudices. In short, it is viewed as a sedative to lull someone into believing things the rational mind rejects.

With all these sorts of ideas floating around, faith can appear un-fathomable, bewildering, and difficult to deal with. As the well-respected Nanamoli Thera once noted:

> Sheer ignorance, gullibility, credulity, belief, faith, trust, confidence, certainty, knowledge—set out like that, the words seem to form a sort of spectrum with faith (most disputed of all the shades) somewhere in the middle.[1]

---

1. Thera, *Does Saddha Mean Faith?*, 18.

In fact, in the Western Zen world, it would be fair to say that most practitioners don't consider faith important to practice and realization. In associating faith with theism, some of us may even think it useless or irrelevant to a Buddhist life. We either disregard, downgrade or criticize faith according to how negative our experience has been with it in our own lives and/or our nation's history.

But, and this is a very crucial point, is the faith that we have in our minds actually the same faith that Zen (and Buddhism in general) speak of? Are we ascribing to Zen faith characteristics that it does not actually have? This is important to ask at this time in Western practice because we seem to be at the point where the lotus has grafted successfully enough for us to make the kind of decisions which can significantly affect its future direction. Enough time has passed for us to review the Zen journey in the West and to weigh up the pros and cons of certain practices and attitudes.

This includes the common but unexamined habit of giving faith a bad name without really realizing what it entails in Zen practice. To our detriment, many of us ascribe Judeo-Christian understandings to faith which do not align with Zen ones. Essentially, then, this means that the crime of emotional irrationalism and irrelevancy has been pinned on the wrong suspect. Even worse, trusted, and authentic sources of authority, Zen ancestors and sutras, have often been stifled whenever faith enters the scene. Redacted and winnowed, they have been, for the most part, effectively prevented from speaking about a doctrinally sound and legitimate tool of realization mentioned in a stunningly large number of sutras. This has been to Zen's detriment and has generally resulted in an unwittingly reductionist view of what actually constitutes Zen practice. The result is that we have been missing a valuable and effective tool for awakening.

Of course, there's nothing inherently wrong with presenting the Dharma in an accessible manner that people of our time can relate to, and to reshape older approaches into new ones. If something is harmful, ineffective, or unnecessary, it may be best to discard it. We use some things from the past and not others. Zen, like any other school of Buddhism, can only continue if its practices and insights are relevant and practice-friendly to each new generation.

Yet by taking the easy road and avoiding anything remotely resembling faith, especially in historical and written sources, we can miss, or skew genuine and deep insights gained by our own spiritual ancestors, most of whom spoke of faith as an integral part of their practice. We do not do justice to our lineages and masters when we ignore faith or override it with our own biased lenses because we prevent them from speaking freely to us.

My point here is that, in thinking faith is x, we (with all good intentions) transform it into y for ease of use in this century. So, for example, we redact the word faith from traditional teachings or use more accessible (but not as fully encompassing) words such as trust or confidence. The problem with this is that some of our modern assumptions and interpretations can, and have been, conspicuously cherry-picked. Moreover, sometimes they've been completely erroneous. If faith is not x but, in fact, something else, y will never be entirely correct, holistic, or inclusive.

But, and this is the point of writing this book, how many of us are fully aware of this? We in the West know about meditation and mindfulness but do we know about faith and its role in Zen? Why do many of us not recognize that both Eihei Dogen and Bojo Jinul, two giants of Zen in Japan and Korea respectively, considered faith a core component of their practice? Moreover, they were not alone. Other Zen masters such as Hakuin Ekaku, Torei Enji, Wonhyo Taesa and Dahui Zonggao also stressed the usefulness of faith.

In fact, faith and enlightenment have been inextricably entwined in Zen from early times. In the ninth century Dazhu Huihai even went so far as to say to his followers that if they did not have faith in the teaching and diligently practice accordingly, he really didn't know what would happen to them. For many great masters, generating faith in the reality of one's inherent Buddhahood was the necessary cause for achieving not only enlightenment but authority and authenticity of practice.

The classic story concerning the legitimacy of choosing Dajian Huineng as the Sixth Ancestor of Zen clearly illustrates the fact that faith is essential and necessary to truly understand Zen. In this well-known narrative, Huineng's master, Daman Hongren (the fifth ancestor of Zen), decided that Huineng would take his place as the next master, and as proof of the authority he invested in him, gave him his cloak and bowl as symbols of dharma transmission. Huineng then secretly left due to controversy over his appointment.

When one of the monastery's monks caught up with him, Huineng threw his cloak and bowl on a rock and said, "This cloak represents faith; if it is in your power to lift it, I will let you have it." The monk tried to lift it, but it was as unmovable as a mountain. This illustrates the fact that, unlike

Huineng, he could not fully embody faith and for this reason, could not inherit the buddha-seal. As Dogen commented:

> The transmission of the Dharma and the robe [a symbol of a Buddhist monastic], is regarded as proof of true faith, by means of which one buddha authorizes the succession of the Dharma to another buddha . . .[2]

For this argument, whether this story is true or not is neither here nor there. Its message, however, isn't. And that is, that faith and realization are inextricably intertwined.

In light of its importance, then, it is imperative that we begin to learn and understand Zen faith so that a balanced understanding of the Way can be achieved. It would be a shame, therefore, if we let our pre-conceived notions and prejudices prevent us from using faith in all its manifestations purely out of ignorance or because we are unduly influenced by our own unease with the topic.

2. See Kimura, "Faith and Enlightenment in Dogen's Shobogenzo," 156.

3

Faith In Buddhism In General

THE BUDDHIST WORLD HAS a diversity of opinions about faith. It has been variously described as right view, suchness, confidence, trust, aspiration, an act of will, *prajna* (wisdom), understanding, devotion, reverence, conviction, discernment, mutual confidence, and confirmation. There are a few things, however, that are more likely to be agreed upon.

The first is that at some point in Buddhist practice faith plays a part. This is not the view of a minority. Throughout the history of Buddhism, an astonishing number of sutras from both the Theravada and Mahayana tradition have proclaimed this fact.

In the Anguttara Nikaya (The Numerical Discourses) the Buddha instructs a layman saying that there are five things which a Buddha necessarily possesses—faith, endeavor, right thought, concentration, and wisdom. Consequently, a lack of faith equates with "waning in the dharma-discipline proclaimed by the Wayfarer" (the Buddha).

The Mahaprajnaparamita Shastra (Treatise on the Perfection of Great Wisdom) states that if we have pure faith, we can enter the Buddha Way. If we do not, then we cannot. It points out that faith is the capability for wisdom and wisdom is the capability for the accomplishment of the Buddha's teaching. In simple terms, faith is the condition for entering the Way and without it, it is beyond our reach.

Fazang, the Third Ancestor in the Huayan or Flower Garland School (a school which has had a strong influence on Zen), commented on the importance of faith as the foundational cornerstone of the Way:

> ...faith is the primary foundation for all kinds of practices. All practices arise from resolute faith. Therefore, faith is listed first and is made the departure point. If resolute faith is absent, even if there is much understanding, it is only confused thinking . . . because understanding without faith does not advance to practice . . .[1]

Similarly, in the Zhiguan Fuxing Zhuan Hongjue (Commentary on the Great Calming and Contemplation), Fifth Ancestor of the Tientai tradition, Zhanran, stated that faith is the foundation of practice. He stressed that from faith practice must arise since faith is understood as the starting point and the very basis of religious practice.

This relationship between faith and enlightenment also provides the central focus for specific Mahayana sutras such as the Vajracchedika Prajnaparamita Sutra (Diamond Sutra). In this sutra, Subhuti, one of the ten great disciples of Shakyamuni Buddha and foremost in the understanding of emptiness, asked the Buddha whether in "future ages, when this scripture is proclaimed amongst those beings destined to hear it, will any conceive within their minds a sincere, unmingled faith?" The Buddha answered:

> Have no such apprehensive thought. Even at the remote period of five centuries subsequent to the Nirvana of the Tathagata, there will be many disciples . . . assiduously devoted to good works. These, hearing this Scripture proclaimed, will believe in its immutability and will conceive within their minds a pure, unmingled faith. Besides, it is important to realize that faith thus conceived, is not exclusively in virtue of the individual thought of any particular Buddha, but because of its affiliation with the universal thought of all the myriad buddhas throughout the infinite ages. Therefore, among the beings destined to hear this Scripture proclaimed, many, by the Dhyana Paramita, will intuitively conceive a pure and virtuous faith.

This suggests that whenever the Way-seeking mind arises so does faith and vice versa. This means that realization in any shape or form involves faith and this stands true at any time or place. So, while it is perhaps surprising to Western practitioners, faith is nonetheless an important element of the teachings of the Buddha, though the type and nature of faith can be perceived differently for different schools.

In Theravada Buddhism, for example, there has been debate about whether faith precedes wisdom or whether they occur concomitantly.

---

1. Park, *Buddhist Faith and Sudden Enlightenment*, 13.

Earlier modern interpretations tended to favor seeing faith and wisdom or knowledge as separate, with faith replaced by the latter. Faith was treated as a sort of prerequisite for religious action since it was considered to precede other faculties and virtues and decrease as wisdom increases. According to this logic, it is impossible for faith to be an essential quality. It plays an optional role at best. This faith model can be termed the Linear Diminishing Role approach.[2] Philosophers of religion such as Kulatissa Nanda Jayatilleke exemplify this view.

A variant on this theme, the Linear Non-diminishing Role approach argues for the complete reverse. That is, faith increases with knowledge so that when a maximum of knowledge is reached there is a maximum of faith.[3] Benimadhab Barua, scholar of ancient Indian languages, Buddhism and law, for example, made the observation that the deeper the conviction, the stronger the expression of faith. So, while the relationship between faith and knowledge is linear, knowledge does not replace faith. Rather than being optional, therefore, faith is an absolute necessity if wisdom is to be developed.

More recent models have taken a Non-Linear Non-Diminishing Role approach. While it agrees that faith is different from knowledge and does not appear only at the beginning of the Path, greater emphasis is placed on the fact that faith changes in nuance and depth throughout the spiritual journey. Moreover, it contends that faith not only motivates and helps strengthen other virtuous qualities it is commensurate with their development. In other words, faith may start off as an ordinary trust or confidence in the pursuit of knowledge or wisdom, but it then develops into a firmer conviction.

Faith, therefore, is not just a mental attitude or acuity but an outcome of direct experience which develops into a full faculty. As such, faith is not a pre-requisite for wisdom but a co-requisite which develops parallel to it and which results in awakening. Researcher Senevi Aturupana is representative of this approach.

Zen, as I will explain in the following chapters, considers faith to both precede wisdom and occur concurrently with it. In fact, some Zen schools consider the two synonymous and interchangeable since faith is one with practice and enlightenment as well as a means to both. It encompasses all

2. Aturupana, *Saddha: An Analytical Study of Its Role*, 221.

3. Aturupana, *Saddha: An Analytical Study of Its Role*, 53, 222.

the approaches to faith mentioned above but also acknowledges that faith and knowledge can be one and the same.

Secondly, while faith in Buddhism has commonalities with theistic faith it is usually considered to be different to the faith most commonly perceived in the West. Faith in the West is popularly seen as only the intellectual acceptance of something without direct knowledge or proof of it. That is, it is belief without reason or even in the face of all reason so that where there are reasons, evidence and argument, faith is not needed. In fact, for some, faith can even be a more ennobling virtue the less reason they have to believe.[4] Both of these are what comes to mind when many Westerners think of faith.

On the other hand, faith is also commonly seen as a positive emotional response to someone or something. This position is also taken by Buddhism which sees it is an attitude or affective state or a special kind of trust that involves hope. It is a type of practical commitment toward certain ways of acting. In his Pancaskandhaprakarana (Discussion of the Five Aggregates), Buddhist philosopher Vasubandhu (fourth to fifth century CE) defines faith as a firm conviction, desire, and serenity of consciousness towards action, its results, the beneficial and the Triple Gem.[5] Faith is thus linked to a disposition to behavior aimed at realized knowledge and practice of some sort.

Reflecting this, Buddhist texts focus on it as a state of trust, confidence, affection, and devotion inspired by the Triple Gem. Faith is not something that fills the gap left by evidence and reason. Rather, it is something necessary to find them.[6] Through such things as listening to teachers and sutras, testing, reasoning, and experience, we find justification for our faith. This means that faith in Buddhism is not an intellectual affair per se but a sense of experiential learning, ongoing engagement, and anticipation.

The message of the Saddharmapundarika Sutra (Lotus Sutra) is typical of this attitude of open learning, trust, and hope. Numerous times in this sutra the Buddha reassures his listeners that they can firmly believe in the reliability of his words. In fact, in many Mahayana sutras there is a special ending in which a long teaching has been given and those present in the audience depart in joyous faith with the intention of incorporating their new-found understanding into their daily lives.

4. See Carpenter, "Faith Without God in Nagarjuna," 317.

5. Vasubandhu, *Seven Works of Vasubandhu*, 67.

6. See Carpenter, "Faith Without God in Nagarjuna," 320.

Chapter 3 of the sutra describes the jubilant response of Shariputra who, after listening to the Buddha's teaching, realizes the truth of buddha nature.

> Now hearing Buddha's gentle voice, profound and most refined, expounding the pure Law, my heart is filled with joy, my doubts and regrets are ended, as I rest in real Wisdom, assured of becoming Buddha" . . . On this all departed, rejoicing greatly that they had heard the preaching of Shakyamuni.

Mahayana sutras contain numerous expressions like this which refer to an adept's willingness to have faith in the Buddha's teachings. After the Buddha had finished teaching the Maharatnakuta Sutra (Sutra of the Heap of Jewels) the lay-woman Gangottara and everyone else in attendance were said to be jubilant over the Buddha's teaching. They "accepted it with faith and began to follow it with veneration."

In the Pali Canon, this firm and calm conviction engendered by listening to the Buddha is represented by a term mentioned previously, pasada or perfect faith. After the Buddha had given a teaching in the Adittapariyaya Sutta (Fire Sermon), Uggatasarira (a brahmin in attendance) said to the Blessed One, "Excellent, Gotama! From today forth please accept me as your lifelong disciple; I put my faith in you."

This attitude of trust and commitment is considered especially essential at the beginning of Buddhist practice. Trusting in a teacher or the Way functions as an impetus to start on the Path, and acting on that trust provides us with experiential confirmation. These conative aspects of faith are very important because, without intention and will, enactment of the Dharma does not occur.

In Zen it is generally thought that just because faith appears at the beginning of the liberating process, this does not mean it then has no further function other than enabling a person to take their first steps. Rather, it is an intrinsically precious quality to be continuously cultivated.[7] Consequently, we can find two notions of faith in Zen—one at the beginning of the Path (as in it represents the necessary mind state for entering the gate of the Buddha-way) and one at the end, so to speak (as in the ultimate state of mind attesting to the truth).[8]

7. Giustarinin, "Faith and Renunciation in Early Buddhism," 166–167.

8. Taishūkan Shoten, *Comprehensive Dictionary of The Zen Lineage*, 603.

This brings in a third aspect which is particular to Mahayana Buddhism, and that is, that faith is given. This innate faith is suchness or the one mind. Wonhyo, one of the leading thinkers, writers, and commentators of the Korean Buddhist tradition, explained that the one mind has faith as its function or natural expression which means that faith is always grounded in the reality of suchness because it is suchness itself.

In other words, realizing the truth and having deep faith in buddha nature is enlightenment itself. It carries the same meaning as absolute, innate faith, which is equivalent to enlightenment. This means, then, that faith is an expression of that which is given. In other words, it is innate faith within a person which makes us search for realization, and it is this which we confirm whenever we enact faith. It is both the goal and the Way.

Lastly, there is a fourth aspect of likely agreement—that since faith is an act and an attitude, it is also a potential virtue that becomes awakened by the Buddha's teachings. In other words, it is the result of a deliberate choice to adopt a contemplative attitude regarding the phenomenal world and renunciation, and consequently, a wise surrendering to this attitude.[9] This is why faith is considered a virtue because it leads to greater concentration, wisdom, and ethical conduct, which in turn strengthens faith even further. It is not just a concept, belief, or a sense of initial trust but an active virtue which plays a significant functional role in the daily life of a practicing Buddhist.[10]

In the Mahaparinirvana Sutra (Sutra of the Great Decease), the Buddha pointed out that there are two causal factors for the rise of faith, namely, faith arises out of listening to the Dharma, and this listening is itself grounded in faith. Faith and knowledge are inextricably entwined and so are faith, practice and resulting virtue. So, faith is the access to the path and its goal and just like wisdom, a transcendent quality embracing the whole of practice.

Thus, if we see faith as a necessary cause, it is one of many virtuous conditions upon which enlightenment absolutely depends. That is, for realization to occur, faith must always be present whenever enlightenment is. If it is not, neither is realization.

The sticking point for Zen in all of this is whether faith alone is sufficient for enlightenment. As mentioned previously, historically speaking, faith is seen by all traditions as something that just has to be there at some

9. Giustarinin, "Faith and Renunciation in Early Buddhism," 175, 177.

10. Aturupana, *Saddha: An Analytical Study of Its Role,* 222–23.

point for realization to occur. There may be many other factors at play, but faith is one of them.

What causes disagreement, then, is whether just by itself it is enough (or sufficient) to result in enlightenment. According to the late scholar Lal Mani Joshi, Buddhist scholar and Professor of Religious Studies, one way in which early Mahayana differed (and claimed superiority) from Theravada was the theory of authority as realization by faith only. What did he mean by liberation by faith alone? If we understand the difference between a necessary and sufficient cause, we can understand differing attitudes to the importance of faith.

A sufficient cause is something which is enough for another thing to happen. If we are hungry, for example, we eat. In and of itself, just that is enough or sufficient to make us eat. Yet sometimes we eat for reasons other than hunger. We might be seeking emotional relief or perhaps because it is polite to do so. Eating can certainly happen without hunger. It doesn't have to be there whenever eating is. Nevertheless, it is still true that being hungry is sufficient in and of itself to make me eat. Just that can be enough.

Longmen Foyan, a Zen master from the ninth century, taught that if our faith is sufficient, then even if we did nothing, we'd arrive at realization. If our faith is sufficient, he stressed, then we'd need say nothing at all. We just know because in and of itself, faith enables us to transcend the small and separate self.

Other Zen teachers have also confirmed the sufficiency of faith. Enro Oryu, the twenty-second abbot of Koshoji Temple in Uji, stressed the essential role of faith. He told the story of a man who misread the Japanese characters in a passage of the Vajracheddika Sutra (Diamond Sutra). Instead of correctly interpreting them as "unsupported by anything is the mind produced," he read "a small pan with no holes." Yet due to his faith, he experienced a deep, religious understanding.

This was not blind faith in some outside deity or object. The faith mentioned in this situation was a complete embodiment and trusting of the awareness which comes with realization. Thus, when he discerned his error and re-read the passage correctly but self-consciously, awareness and insight were absent.[11] His conceptual mind had got in the way.

As we would expect, "faith-based" Mahayana traditions such as Nichiren and Pure Land view the sufficiency of faith very positively. The Saddharmapundarika Sutra (Lotus Sutra), the main text of the Nichiren sect,

---

11. Sakurai, "In the Zen Sect," 138.

states that those who listen to the Cosmic Buddha's teachings are free from the delusions and the miseries of life. The sutra reminds adherents that it is through faith that we must enter his teaching. If we turn in faith to the Buddha, the sutra reassures us, the Tathagata will not deceive us because we can "gain entrance" through faith alone.

Pure Land, the most popular form of Buddhism in Japan, relies on the sufficiency of faith in other-power. If a person recites the name of this other-power, Amida Buddha, with enough faith, devotion, and single-mindedness, this faith will enable them to be reborn in his Pure Land. This occurs either metaphorically as a state of enlightenment or after death in the celestial abode of Amida described in Mahayana sutras.

This involves complete reliance on faith alone or *shinjin* (true entrusting). Shinjin is a combination of faith, complete confidence in the efficacy of the teachings, and pasada, the mental equanimity attained at an advanced level of the path. It is the total involvement or embodiment of faith which is synonymous with the power of Amida. The Avatamsaka Sutra (Flower Garland Sutra) states that:

> . . . Buddha gives a power to faith that leads people to the Pure Land, a power that purifies them, a power that protects them from self-delusion. Even if they have faith only for a moment, when they hear Buddha's name praised all over the world, they will be led to his Pure Land.

Likewise, the Sukhavativyuha Sutra (Infinite Life Sutra) teaches that if anyone hearing the name of Amida Buddha is encouraged to call upon that name in perfect faith, they will share in the Buddha's teaching.

If we view faith in this manner, as enough or sufficient in itself to cause enlightenment, then it is also more likely that we take the view that faith is saving. Contrastingly, other schools of Buddhism do not consider faith strong enough in and of itself to engender nirvana. Certainly, in early Buddhism, faith was never regarded as sufficient for the attainment of nirvana. In Mahayana, it depends on the school, sutra, and teacher.

The Mahaprajnaparamita Shastra (Treatise on the Perfection of Great Wisdom), for example, suggests that while we enter the great sea of Buddha's teaching by faith, it is only through wisdom that we become enlightened. Since faith in the teachings or a teacher is essential at the beginning of the Path, it occurs when a person listens to a teacher or reads sacred text.

In other words, there is some sort of impetus to begin walking the Path. This arouses faith which leads to practice and ultimately the direct experience of enlightenment i.e., the state in which faith is replaced with knowledge. In the Pusa Yingluo Benye Jing (Sutra of the Garland of a Bodhisattva's Primary Karmas) the Buddha states, "I begin with faith and vows, and will end with great wisdom."

This model presents aspects or levels of development, namely, faith, understanding, practice, realization, and consolidation. Firstly, there is faith engendered through listening to a teacher. Secondly, academic scholarship or an intellectual understanding. This is followed by putting what one has learned into practice to test out its truth and utility. The aim of this stage is to make the application of the Buddha's teachings a habitual practice. The next most important mode is the wordless and intuitive realization of the truth. Lastly, there is the full integration of the initial insight into all activities. In this final stage, a person moves beyond kensho, our insight and awareness event, without ever clinging to it.

Anyone with this view considers faith as both secondary and prior to knowledge. The Satapancasatka (Matrceta's Hymn to the Buddha) says that although we may associate with the Dharma out of faith, we only truly know something when we understand it. So, although faith precedes this, understanding is still the chief of the two. Consequently, faith is separate and different from first-hand knowledge.

If, however, we consider faith and knowledge as either equal partners or synonymous with each other, then we agree with the Mahaparinirvana Sutra (Sutra of the Great Decease). It points out that, although there are innumerable practices that lead to enlightenment, if we teach faith, then that includes all of them. In the Avatamsaka Sutra (Flower Garland Sutra) it is stated that the presence of faith is so important that the Bodhisattva Diamond Treasury only begins to teach the Dharma after he has ascertained its presence in the audience of listeners.

Why is it that without faith, the bodhisattva felt his words would fall on deaf ears? It has to do with the nature of dependent origination which dictates that an effect can only manifest when all the necessary conditions are complete and present. Even when the Buddha himself gave teachings the necessary conditions had to be there. This is why sutras begin with the discourse marker, "Thus have I heard."

The significance of this phrase is that it shows that the *liu chengjiu* or six accomplishments are present. That is, faith, hearing, time, teacher, location, and assembly. "Thus I have heard" indicates not only the speaker's faith that what follows is truly Dharmically correct, but that the audience has the proper mind-frame i.e., the faith to receive them. As the Mahapra-jnaparamita Shastra (Treatise on the Perfection of Great Wisdom) states, if we have faith, we say "Thus" but if we have no faith we say, "Not thus."

Yet while faith is often described in many sutras as the initial step that gets us on the Way, it is also seen as continuous, total practice itself. This reflects two general approaches in Buddhism. As Dogen pointed out, prac-tice is not only a means to enlightenment it is itself enlightenment as well. Anytime practice occurs it is simultaneously an act of faith, which is also an act of realizing or enacting buddha nature. In this way, faith is both the goal and the method, both necessary to realization and enough or sufficient.

Thus, if we were to speak in very broad terms, although all three atti-tudes can be found in all vehicles of Buddhism, later schools generally tend to focus more on faith as a constant throughout practice than earlier ones who more often than not view it as an initial step on the Path. The former tends to see faith as referring to the entire chain of cause and effect whereas the latter sees it as a discrete stage.

If we look at faith within just the Zen tradition, we can see that, again in a very general sense, two broad views of faith exist. One centers on faith in original enlightenment whereas another starts from faith in attaining enlightenment and returning to our original nature. Soto Zen tends to see faith as simultaneously both the goal and the way whereas Rinzai generally views faith as an attitude of trust and/or an initial step towards knowledge. In other words, although there are many commonalities between the two, Soto Zen tends to be based on enlightenment from the beginning in con-trast to Rinzai's enlightenment with a beginning.

Since they hold these differing views, it is no surprise that they have also tended to emphasize differing faith approaches to realization. Soto has historically favored enactment of faith in the form of shikantaza (also known as silent illumination or just sitting). Keizan Jokin, the second great founder of Soto in Japan, stated that just-sitting meditation based on faith is the fullest form of true enlightenment. Rinzai Zen mainly uses koans as a method by which to engender absolute trust in one's own buddha nature. Based on faith in original enlightenment, kensho, an insight event, is, in turn, considered the actualization of that faith.

Sung Bae Park, Professor of Asian Philosophy and Religions, calls these two approaches doctrinal and patriarchal faith. Doctrinal faith involves be-coming a buddha, whereas patriarchal faith expresses the affirmation that we are already Buddha. The first is a preliminary to enlightenment, while the latter is itself enlightenment.

Doctrinal faith makes use of a subject-object relationship in that a practitioner has faith *in* the Buddha, Dharma, and Sangha. This dualism is eventually overcome through practice and kensho. Patriarchal faith, however, expresses an essence-function relationship. Faith is a function of enlightenment rather than a preliminary to it. In other words, faith does not require an object to believe in but is a natural function or expression of our originally enlightened Mind. This is faith *as* Buddha.

As we can see, there are two major directions in which faith flows in Zen—as a preliminary step aimed at enabling a person to eventually become a buddha and the constant practice of being Buddha. The first is most probably familiar to most Zen practitioners whereas the second is more likely to be either less well-known or explicitly emphasized only in certain schools of Zen. Subsequent chapters will focus on the necessity of both in Zen practice.

4

Faith's Journey

So how have these interpretations of faith, in particular Zen faith, come about in the West? One thing that immediately jumps out from the history books is the general tendency of Western Buddhists to follow in the footsteps of our predecessors. Many of us have accepted, sometimes unquestioningly, perceptions and views given to us by our predecessors. Following in a teacher's footsteps is, of course, unremarkable, and not automatically problematic. In fact, to actually have a teacher to follow is a rare luxury in the West.

In the case of faith, however, we have unwittingly passed on a penchant for seeing both Buddhism and the Buddha's experience of enlightenment through the lenses of the ideals which arose from European enlightenment and romanticism, and American transcendentalism. Again, there is nothing inherently negative about these. The result of over a hundred years of this approach, however, is the high level of automaticity with which we associate Buddhism with certain things and not others.

That is, we group Buddhism together with scientific rationalism, individual enlightenment, psychological empowerment, and humanism, and not with aspects which we think appear incompatible with these. As Bhikkhu Bodhi once pointed out, when we first encounter Buddhism it appears to Western eyes a freethinker's delight—realistic, scientific, and undogmatic. Again, in and of itself, there's no problem at all with this. If these lenses are the only ones we use or the airing of alternate viewpoints are not presented, however, that can be to our detriment. This has been the case for perceptions of faith and faith practices which are commonly skewed negatively.

This colonial-era orientalist bias first arose in the nineteenth century when early Western pioneers of Buddhism began to present Buddhism in a way that suggested it was the religion most suited to a progressive western culture. They set about reinforcing the idea that the Buddha's injunction to test and question was what set it apart from the more irrational aspects of the Christian faith.

Buddhism was interpreted as a system based on reason, self-control, and scientific experientialism, and was directly opposed to ritual, superstition, primitive faith, and irrational devotion. Professor Lakshmi Narasu of Madras Christian College proudly proclaimed in 1907 that of Buddhism alone can it be affirmed that it is free from all fanaticism.

However, given that Zen is maintained and propagated by humans and humans are susceptible to error, it stands to reason that at some point in Zen's history, mistakes were sure to be made. And made they have been, sometimes in a heartbreakingly unethical fashion. Yet such a picture of Buddhist rationality has been painted that even today a certain amount of cognitive dissonance and astonishment occurs when we consider such things as Zen's role in World War Two or Ashin Wirathu (*The Face of Buddhist Terror*) on the cover of Time Magazine. The knee-jerk degree of incredulity in the West that such things could happen in Buddhism has at times seemed naively out of proportion to reality.

In terms of faith, therefore, if we apply Lakshmi's statement and others like it without scrutiny, our impression of Zen Buddhism might be that it is completely faithless and has no time for anything to do with faith. If we consider this in terms of blind and unfounded faith this is indeed the case. If we consider this in terms of other types of faith, it is blatantly untrue.

Yet because many of us naturally went down the Western tunnel of interpretation set for us by our predecessors, very few of us know this, and that in addition to faith in the Buddha, faith as the Buddha has always played an important role in Zen practice.

In fact, it is the latter that most delineates Zen views of faith from those of Theravada. Generally speaking, two historical forms of faith can be distinguished in Buddhism—that of early Buddhism and the later Mahayana. Both have varying views about the role and efficacy of faith. Some early twentieth-century European scholars, such as Louis de La Vallee-Poussin, Arthur Berriedale Keith and Caroline Rhys Davies, did not always distinguish the two sufficiently. Nevertheless, Mahayana practice in the unique form of faith as the Buddha is a concrete historical fact.

It might also be that in our Western search for a demystified and demythologized Buddhism, we have unwittingly allowed for a meditation-centric Zen which somehow sidelines faith in general. This is another example of the lack of importance placed upon faith in Zen as a by-product of modernist interpretations. That is, since meditation was interpreted as a kind of mental technology which could be abstracted out of its ideological context, it became a practice recommended for everyone. This has meant that modern Buddhism has generally dismissed certain practices (such as faith) deemed non-essential.

This is a departure from tradition in which contextualized meditation is only one of many spiritual activities. Yet for many Zen practitioners, practice automatically equates with meditation. This widespread assumption can unfortunately imply that those Buddhists who have alternative practices have never really "practiced" their religion. As noted in *Tricycle: The Buddhist Review*:

> Among Western convert Buddhists, there has always been a sharp division, exacerbated by prejudice and misunderstanding, between [the practice of faith-based Buddhists such as] Nichiren Buddhists and those pursuing approaches based on quiet sitting. Meditation-oriented Buddhists often think of Nichiren Buddhists (if they think of them at all) with little real knowledge and even with condescension. The same is true in how they view Pure Land Buddhists.[1]

Indeed, there is considerable irony in the fact that, despite the Western impression of Zen as the meditation school, most Zen temples in Japan function as social centers and places to conduct rituals rather than meditation. Nonetheless, this primacy of meditation has, intentionally or unintentionally, shunted faith (or what we think Zen faith is) out of the picture.

This brings up yet another facet of the faith story in Zen—the generally secular and rationalist tendency in the West for us to feel uncomfortable with anything seen as magical or non-empirical. As a by-product of Buddhist Modernism, faith can often be lumped in with other aspects of Buddhism deemed irrelevant and irrational, or an unnecessary cultural accretion no longer needed in modern life.

1. Cooper, "Understanding Nichiren Buddhism," para. 2.

This is exemplified in the ways in which Asian Buddhism has been re-oriented for a Western audience in terms of a return to the "original" or "pure" Buddhist teachings. In doing this, the West has usually sought to discover certain universal truths of the Dharma. Consequently, many Buddhists in the West erroneously perceive that a pure form of Buddhism exists which can be distilled from its cultural baggage.

One result of this is that some of us in the West can be carelessly eager to jump upon sections of the Dharma or practices which we think give support to our belief that irrational or superstitious elements have accrued along the way in the historical development of Buddhism and that underneath these a pure Zen can be found.

An excellent illustrative example which comes to mind is Dogen's admonition in the Bendowa (Discourse on the Practice of the Way) to refrain from certain practices such as incense offerings, prostrations, the *nembutsu* (reciting the Buddha Amida's name as mantra), repentance practices or sutra reading. This is often cited as proof that certain traditional practices are extraneous and superfluous add-ons.

The problem with this is that by selectively focusing on certain texts and practices to the detriment of others, we can ignore or be completely unaware of information which could provide either an alternative view or a more balanced one, especially about faith practices. In this case, the fact that every one of the ritual practices that Dogen dismissed in the Bendowa were prescribed and encouraged by him in great detail in his other writings. This includes faith and faith practices such as devotional acts of reverence and gratitude.

In the Kuyo Shobutsu (Making Offerings to Buddhas) section of the Bendowa Dogen quotes Nagarjuna, a second-century Indian master:

> If you want the effect of being a buddha, recite one verse of praise,
> chant one refuge, burn a pinch of incense, or offer one flower. Even
> with such a small practice, you will certainly become a buddha.[2]

Although Dogen stressed that meditation was *the* authentic practice, he was very clear about the importance of not dismissing others, including devotional ones.

In Kie Sanbo (Taking Refuge in the Three Treasures), he particularly praised the Saddharmapundarika Sutra (Lotus Sutra) and it is highly likely that he was motivated by its emphasis upon the efficacy of even small acts of

2. Dogen, *Treasury of the True Dharma Eye*, 237, 828.

reverence. The sutra teaches that whenever someone shows sincere faith in the Buddha by performing a good deed, no matter how small (even coloring an image of the Buddha) this act sets them on the path to Buddhahood.

Recent scholarship supports this notion that Dogen was as much a devotee of meditation, as he was a proponent of balance within the teaching and practice of Zen Buddhism. Despite Soto practice being generally almost equated with shikantaza, the main kind of meditation advocated by the Soto Zen school, many other expressions feature just as prominently in his writings.

While he didn't compose a separate chapter on faith in his Shobogenzo (Treasure of the True Dharma Eye), for example, there are many statements about it in various chapters that leave no doubt that it is the basis for the practice of Dogen's Way.[3] So while he only explicitly uses the word faith twice in this text he used many synonyms to refer to other related or synonymous aspects of Zen teaching and practice. The character for belief (shin), for example, was mentioned 185 times in as many as 48 chapters and occurs in the entire work just as often as zazen. Evidently, Dogen didn't hesitate to describe Zen practice in terms of faith, devotion, repentance, prayer, and merits of the Buddhas.[4]

It would seem, therefore, that the assertion of twentieth-century Soto scholars that Dogen rejected syncretic practices in favor of a pure Zen consisting of an exclusive devotion to zazen is not entirely supported. In fact, some modern academics assert that these claims are "nothing more than a projection of the modern Zen academic embarrassment with traditional modes of Buddhist ritual onto the founder of the school."[5]

Important to the above, is the understanding that embarrassment about the role of faith is not confined to Western circles but is widespread in many areas of Buddhism in the East as well. In a clear example of the pizza effect,[6] modernist and colonialist cherry-picking was transmitted *back*

---

3. Cook, *How to Raise an Ox,* 22–23.

4. Kubovcakova, "Believe It or Not," 206–07, 209.

5. See Foulk, "Ritual in Japanese Zen Buddhism," 42.

6. The pizza effect is a tendency for cultures to influence each other in a loop. It occurs when a particular phenomenon is taken to another country, and then following its success abroad, is re-branded in the original country as an authentic, longstanding tradition. Coined by Anthropologist Agehanda Bharati, the term is an analogy to the spread of pizza globally, in particular, between the USA and Italy. The original pizza was a simple, hot-baked bread without any trimmings but became a highly elaborated dish in the US in the 1920s.

to Asia, especially to educated elites. Ironically, then, we can hear Western rationalistic and psychological interpretations (as well as misinterpretations) in the countries from which the West obtained its information about Buddhism in the first place. This gives the mistaken impression that newer interpretations are actually older, original ones when, in fact, some of them are recent imports.

Nevertheless, the fact remains that despite the modern yearning to return to a "pure" Zen (which rejects devotion, sutras, faith, and ritual), it has always been an ahistorical, formless, spiritual entity.[7] It has never existed as such simply because such an essentialized Buddhism is itself another interpretation resultant from its own process of selection.[8]

So, while some of us conceive of religions as intact traditions with clear boundaries, distinct ideologies, and unique histories, sociological and religious studies have long shown that these conceptions fall apart under scrutiny. Modern scholars are now becoming more aware that the lines separating the Sanron sect from Tendai, for example, and Tendai from Pure Land, Pure Land from Zen, Zen from Neo-Confucianism, and elite from popular are by no means as clear as was once thought.[9] This is because religious traditions develop and exist in relation to one another and their particular contexts.[10] In reality, the local practices of culture and religion are rarely as pure and unmixed as their members would like to think they are. In fact, all religious cultures are syncretic and there is no such thing as a non-syncretic religious tradition.[11] Indeed, in every religion that has moved across cultural borders, syncretic phenomena can be found.

Zen in the West is no exception. It might appear to us that our version of Zen is the "real" Zen but that does not erase the fact that it is, nonetheless, a syncretic result of our own western perceptions just as Japanese and Chinese Zens are a product of their environments as well.

I would strongly argue, then, that, despite perceptions otherwise, Zen faith is entirely applicable to the Western context. This is precisely because it is no different to anything else in Zen that has been molded and utilized. It worked in days long past, and it still works now, even if we shape it to fit

---

7. See Foulk, "Ritual in Japanese Zen Buddhism," 36.

8. Payne, "Intertwined Sources of Modernist Opposition to Ritual," para. 11.

9. Sharf, *Coming to Terms with Chinese Buddhism*, 3.

10. Bender and Cadge, "Constructing Buddhism(s)," 229.

11. Nye, *Religion: The Basics*, 53.

our modern needs. If we are fair to faith and consider it without prejudice, it will stand us in good stead.

To do this, it must be recognized that not only are many common views of Zen faith still erroneous but that these pervasive negative perceptions have at times unwittingly perpetuated inaccurate accounts of Zen practice itself. Despite the fact, for example, that sacramental practices in Zen have always been present, even (or precisely) when they were most vehemently repudiated,[12] the West remains convinced that Zen eschews ritual and form.

The British diplomat and historian George Sansom confidently claimed in 1931, for example, that "a Zen teacher reads no sutras, he performs no ceremonies, worships no images, and he conveys instruction to his pupil not by long sermons but by hints and indications."[13] One wonders if he had ever entered any *zendo* or seen Zen practice at all. One look at a Zen Liturgical document or Zen practitioners bowing would've been enough to shatter his claim entirely.

Even twenty-nine years later in 1960 similar over-generalizations were still being perpetuated. In his preface to the fifth volume of *Zen and Zen Classics*, Reginald Horace Blyth, an associate of D.T. Suzuki and other Buddhist practitioners who introduced Zen to Western audiences, wrote that "Zen draws us to it for many reasons . . . No dogmas, no ritual, no mythology, no church, no priest, no holy book."[14] Zen literature in the West has espoused these kinds of categorical and unsupportable statements to such an extent that we are still living the legacy of this particular perception today.

It is not surprising, then, that a sense of unease about faith continues. This sense of discomfort has threaded its way insidiously into Western academia in the form of unease over the presence of Buddhist scholar-practitioners. This too exerts a degree of influence upon research interests and perceptions of legitimacy about faith practices.

The early pioneers of Buddhist Studies in the West were not Buddhists whereas, in the modern era, it is now common for individuals teaching Buddhist Studies in universities to be scholar-practitioners. It has been difficult for some of these scholars to allay the fear that they lack critical

12. Faure, *The Rhetoric of Immediacy*, 305.

13. Sansom, *Japan: A Short Cultural History*, 337.

14. Blyth, *Volume Five Zen and Zen Classics*, 7–8.

distance from Buddhism; that their faith does not influence their neutrality or diminish the acuity and legitimacy of their academic insight.

In *Buddhism, Poststructuralist Thought, Cultural Studies: A Profession of Faith* Edwin Ng prefaced his study with concerns about how seriously a university thesis which mentions faith would be received. He writes:

> Propelling this autoethnographic project is a question of faith. Yet, I've been uncomfortable and afraid of articulating this outright. Why? Much of the discomfort stems from the tensions constituting my subjectivity as a religiously committed Buddhist attempting to understand my faith with and through the secular discourses of cultural studies. Perhaps I'm afraid of the disapproval, or even ridicule I might face in professing the religious inspiration I bring to and discover through academia. But can't this commitment to knowledge also be hospitable to faith, and therefore the possibility that religion or spiritual pursuits may have crucial things to say about those conundrums we grapple with, like ethics, (inter) subjectivity and the body? In tackling these conundrums with Buddhism and poststructuralist thought, I find it irresponsible to pretend that faith does not also support my practice of cultural studies. Hence, by way of an analysis this essay makes a profession of faith.[15]

Ng argues that this lack of attention of critical inattentiveness to the intersections of faith and spirituality has been caused primarily by a conscious or unconscious acceptance of the secularization thesis (that religion would be replaced by secularism) in certain academic circles. In his opinion, this has propelled academia (in this case, cultural studies) headlong in a misguided direction. This would seem generally representative of the kind of reservations some sections of academia have about either expressing faith or its usefulness in an increasingly secular, rationalist world.

To add to this, our unease with practices perceived as unsuited to modernity has, in turn, been further conditioned by the commonplace separation many of us make between Zen practices and sensibilities, and those of faith-based traditions such as Pure Land and Nichiren Buddhisms. Faith is often seen as contrary to Zen because it seems to imply a dualism between a person and the object they have faith in. This may be why an almost implacable demarcation is commonly drawn between Zen as "experiential" and Pure Land as "devotional."

15. Ng, "Buddhism, Poststructuralist Thought, Cultural Studies," 109–110.

This placement of Buddhism into a faith versus experience dichotomy is the unfortunate result of purposeful efforts by early Japanese teachers to introduce a particular view of Zen to the West. D. T. Suzuki, the main proponent of Zen to the West last century, was particularly responsible for what academic Robert Sharf has termed "reconstructed Zen."[16] That is, a Zen which was presented as speculative, intellectual, and self-reliant. Pure Land, on the other hand, was pitched as devotional, emotional, and dependent on the Buddha. Zen represented the intellectual side of Japanese spirituality while Pure Land was the emotional.[17]

Suzuki's comments were clearly filtered through Zen sensibilities, and he reflected a general trend in Zen to read its own presuppositions into Pure Land in order to synthesize its teachings with its own. To this end, Zen was given a privileged position while faith-based traditions were positioned as reinforcing support.[18]

This was bolstered by other experts such as the late Masao Abe, professor in religious studies and interfaith specialist, who promoted the notion that Zen differs from theistic religions primarily because it is built upon awakening, not faith. This is only true if the faith he is talking about is theistic or blind. His interpretation did not give the full story of faith in Buddhism as a whole and sold Pure Land and Zen practices short. As a result, it put faith and its every facet into a sealed box into which it did not belong.

Abe saw faith and enlightenment as two different and contrary things since, by his definition, faith is other-directed (such as to a deity) whereas awakening is self-produced. This definition of faith and faith practices entirely excluded other sorts of non-theistic faith that can be found in Zen. Dogen would most certainly take issue with awakening as produced solely by oneself since he drew upon the support given by the lineage of historical buddhas and ancestors, the cosmic buddhas and bodhisattvas, and the phenomenal world of the environment informed by buddha-dharma.[19]

It also did not reflect Chinese Zen which throughout its history has had a high degree of assimilation between Zen and Pure Land practices so that by the time syncretic Pure Land-Zen practices eventually came to Japan, they had already undergone a long journey of development in China

16. See Sharf, "Whose Zen? Zen Nationalism Revisited," 50.

17. Porcu, *Pure Land Buddhism in Modern Japanese Culture*, 67, 71–74, 159.

18. Porcu, *Pure Land Buddhism in Modern Japanese Culture*, 71–74.

19. Leighton, *Visions of Awakening Space and Time*, 3.

where they were considered a natural and legitimate combination. It is far from the truth, therefore, to assert that Pure Land practice is incompatible with or a corruption of Zen because the appearance of the nembutsu within established Zen institutions is with clear precedent in China.[20]

This was not the case for Japan, however, where, for a variety of reasons, both practices have always been considered incongruous by most Zen schools. Established in 1661 by a group of masters from China, only Obaku Zen (the smallest Zen sect in Japan) fully utilized Pure Land practices, sometimes derogatorily referred to by other sects as Nembutsu Zen.

This has meant that most representations of Pure Land in the West have been filtered through a lens which often frowned upon it as a dualistic and expedient teaching meant only for people of limited physical and mental capacities. Moreover, since Zen totally transcends all forms of dualism and cannot be limited by any philosophical or religious worldview, the common but polemic consensus held by Suzuki and other Japanese proponents in the West was that Zen represents the true root of all forms of Buddhism. As such, it preserves most perfectly the original spirit of Buddhism.

Other schools are bound by their attachment to particular sutras and masters but Zen is a transmission outside the scriptures and not reliant on text or doctrine. As such, Zen was sold to the West as not just a type of Buddhism, it was Buddhism itself.

As with anyone else, Suzuki was perfectly entitled to take his own position on Zen. There is no contention with that basic right. What is problematic is that this particular polemic resulted in a state of affairs where it was considered fruitful to synthesize Pure Land and Zen according to Zen's philosophy.[21] This did not do justice to either and denied the complexity of their religious systems and doctrinal foundations. Nevertheless, the common outcome was the inference that since Pure Land was a kind of inferior Zen suitable to those of lesser ability, it was better to choose Zen. The West, infatuated with the charismatic and knowledgeable Suzuki, drank this in as gospel.

This was despite the fact that many Pure Land texts and teachers both elucidated and demonstrated the efficacy of nembutsu practices. In the Chewu Chanshi Yulu (The Recorded Sayings of Chan Master Jixing Chewu), a Zen-Pure Land syncretic text, Chewu explicitly stated that the Pure Land dharma-gate covers all beings of the three roots i.e., inferior,

---

20. Baskind, "The Nianfo in Obaku Zen," 19.

21. Ingram, "The Zen Critique of Pure Land Buddhism," 196, 200.

middling, and superior, and that there is no level of capability that it does not take in. Yet numerous examples in the past one hundred years tell us that such unambiguous assertions were at times ignored or downplayed by Zen adherents.

The effects of this continue in Zen practice today. We can see this in the way in which contemplation, devotion, meditation, and faith have been categorized as exclusionary activities by most modern Buddhists. This placement of distinct borders around certain practices is the culmination of a historical journey which began in the Edo period (1603 to 1868 CE) when European accounts of Pure Land and Zen sects were sculpted by Christian religious views which judged its own denominations by what seemed *not* to belong to the other.

Reflecting a Protestant-influenced conception of religion which emphasized cognitive, intellectual, doctrinal, and dogmatic aspects, Western theologists favored a Buddhism that "naturally" had sects with very different doctrines and practices. Adding to this, from 1867–1912 the Meiji government was generally hostile to Buddhism (in favour of Shinto) and directed Soto and Rinzai Zen to either have clear differences or merge.

All of this ran contrary to historical fact since for most of the history of Buddhism, devotional practices (invocation, offerings, homage) have not been at odds or even distinctly separated from meditative practices.[22] Our modern affliction to make categories and posit them as exclusive has not stood us in good stead in this case. It has skewed our perceptions of meditation and devotion when, in fact, until quite recently, equating practice, faith and enlightenment has always been the general standard in Buddhist doctrine.[23]

Given all the above, it is no surprise that many of us in the West feel uncomfortable with the word faith. My own unease with it is reflected in the hours I spent trying to think of an appropriate title for this book. I wanted to include the word on the cover, but I didn't want to disenchant readers so that they summarily dismissed it without considering what I had to say. The irony of writing a book about faith yet struggling not to mention it was not lost on me.

As the previous factors indicate, this strong sense of wariness did not originate from a vacuum. It is readily apparent that for many of us Judeo-Christian understandings prevail purely because that is the dominant

22. Grumbach, "Nenbutsu and Meditation," 91.

23. Grumbach, "Nenbutsu and Meditation,"96.

context into which Zen faith has been placed. In the West, this tends to condition much of the discourse about Zen. The origin of our theistic-influenced notion of faith is clear cut.

But it also might be that the lack of clarity in Western Zen around faith has been compounded by the fact that within one text or teaching there may be a variety of uses of the word coupled with contrasting views of its utility. Take *Zen: The Authentic Gate* by my late Dharma Grandfather (my teacher's teacher) Koun Yamada. In the second chapter entitled *The Zen View: Faith-based Spirituality and Experience-based Spirituality* he states:

> . . . we may describe faith-based spirituality as grounded in belief and understanding, whereas experience-based spirituality empha-sizes practice, realization, and actualization . . . unlike faith-based religions, Zen rejects concepts and beliefs as a means of knowing the truth.[24]

Yamada did not believe that Zen was a religion since he drew a divide be-tween it (faith-based spirituality) and Zen (experience-based spirituality). Religion, he states, relies on faith and belief, two terms which in this case suggest knowledge without experience. On the other hand, experience-based spirituality does not emphasize faith at all. This passage suggests Yamada saw faith only as belief without experiential support, that is, either a lesser, preliminary stage of realization or dualistically theistic.

Yet, in a later chapter *Cause and Effect as One* Yamada points out the following:

> So if a person who has just taken up the practice of zazen today *trusts* in the teaching of an authentic teacher and practices as di-rected, even if they are unaware of it, they *embody absolute virtue* that is no different from that of Shakyamuni or Amida Buddha. [my italics][25]

Essentially, then, in one book he has used faith as belief, faith as an initial stage of enlightenment, faith as trust in the Buddha (as represented by a teacher), and faith as a unified, embodied state of realization.

Texts outside the Zen tradition are not immune to this multiplicity of meanings either. A representative example is Karen Armstrong's *Buddha* in which she points out that the Buddha's recognition of himself as the

---

24. Yamada, *Zen: The Authentic Gateway*, 11.
25. Yamada, *Zen: The Authentic Gateway*, 120.

supreme reality, was an act of faith in the human potential, and a trust that nirvana could be proven.

In the Ariyapariyesana Sutta, she notes that the Buddha took care to point out that Alara Kalama's realization was not just "simply out of faith" because he had arrived at nirvana through knowledge and experience. Rather than faith as a purely intellectual assent, he preferred the kind of faith and confidence in the teachings gained through self-confirmed experience. Lastly, Armstrong uses faith as a way of distinguishing people who belong to a particular religion such as those of the Buddhist faith or the Christian faith.

Unfortunately, rather than acclimatizing to the many variants of faith, this diversity of meanings has sometimes been exacerbated by the fact that we often don't know what we don't know. We are all influenced by the limitations of our own knowledge, and we simply may not know of alternative usages and practices of faith.

Long-time readers of Tricycle's *Daily Dharma* emails might remember reading in 2010 the controversial article "Buddhism and Faith" which contained a quote from Hakuun Yasutani. In this article Yasutani gives unequivocal support for Buddhism as a religion, and that the reason for this is the element of faith, without which Buddhism is "mere philosophy." The Buddha attained enlightenment due to inherent buddha nature—the fact that all existence is intrinsically whole. Without unwavering faith in this (which he calls the "heart of the Buddha's teaching"), it is impossible to progress far in our practice.

As expected, many of the comments in reaction to Yasutani were contingent upon an individual's understanding of faith within their own tradition. For example, one objector based his argument on the fact that we are not intrinsically whole, but we can become enlightened by following the Buddhist path out of ignorance, unawareness, and attachment.

This is certainly true from a Theravada viewpoint (and in a general sense from the Rinzai Zen view as well). It reflects faith in the Dharma as a preliminary stage until we become enlightened. This is doctrinally correct and if we take this position Yasutani is wrong. We cannot take faith in the fact that we are already enlightened simply because most of us have not yet abandoned greed, hatred, and ignorance.

Yet if considered from the Mahayana (in particular, Soto Zen) viewpoint of the oneness of cause and effect, Yasutani's observation is absolutely true as well. This is faith as ongoing and manifested buddha nature. This demonstrates that faith is multifaceted, and an awareness of its many meanings is essential to see all sides of the story. It is also interesting to note that while the founder of Sanbo-zen (Yasutani) considered Zen a religion, his successor, Yamada, did not.

To muddy the waters further, in the minds of many, religion and faith go together. So, it is also essential to be clear in our minds about where we stand on religion if we are to properly understand Zen faith. However, and you guessed it, there is even ambiguity when it comes to describing Buddhism itself (and by implication Zen as well). Is it mysticism, a religion, a technique, a spiritual path, a humanist philosophy, or a way of life? Is it rational, scientific, experience-based, therapeutic, a science of mind or a psychology of mind? Is it some, all, or none of these?

In a Shambhala Sun article entitled *Is Buddhism a Religion?* Buddhologist Charles Prebish answered "No," Dzogchen Ponlop Rinpoche, the abbot of Dzogchen Monastery, "Yes," and Zen teacher Joan Sutherland "Kind of." In the Zen is a religion camp we find people such as David Brazier, Head of the Amida Order and President of the International Zen Therapy Institute, the late Reverend Master Jiyu-Kennett of the Order of Buddhist Contemplatives and Hakuun Yasutani, founder of the Sanbo-Zen school.

Its opposite, the Zen is not a religion group, includes the late Alan Watts, Ryoun Yamada, current Abbot of Sanbo-zen, and Brad Warner. Zen teacher and author David Loy even asks in the *Eastern Buddhist* journal, "Is Zen Buddhism?" To make matters even more interesting, in seeking to be flexible and realistic, modern Zen teachers such as Domyo Burk from Bright Way Zen offer both religious Zen and secular Zen. The jury is obviously out on the religion question.

This is not to say, however, that a variety of interpretations is an insurmountable problem since a diversity of meaning is evident in both the Theravada and Mahayana Canons. Although they both differ in their assessment of the extent to which faith fosters realization, they both present faith as legitimately and naturally multi-faceted.

Pasada, for example, denotes faith that is not impassioned, zealous, or irrational. It is, however, joyful and positive spiritual emotion. It is steadfast faith and resolve towards the truth and has been variously translated as to grow clear and bright and to become placid and tranquil. It is marked by a quiet assurance, satisfaction, clarity, awe, veneration, and mental non-disturbance—the kind of enjoyment that comes from peace of mind.

Nalinaksha Dutt, well-known author and scholar, defined it as the serene pleasure arising from unshakeable insight and conviction rooted in the understanding of things as they really are. Accordingly, pasada expresses the idea of purity and clarity since the proper purpose of faith is to cleanse the mind so that our inherent wisdom can shine forth. Unsurprisingly, in the Mahayana tradition, pasada is prominent in such sutras as the Saddharmapundarika Sutra (Lotus Sutra), a sutra outlining faith in universal buddha nature.

Adhimukti (understanding) on the other hand, describes another kind of faith—the feeling of release and freedom that comes from a state of ongoing trust. It exemplifies faith as intention since it not only purifies and strengthens comprehension but elevates it as an engine for continuous self-improvement.

If we look at the Chinese equivalent of this term, *xinjie*, its characters suggest an open and honest attitude that facilitates a true understanding of the nature of reality. This understanding is so clear and deep that its results are threefold: it frees an individual from the confines of the separate self, it enables full embodiment of a knowledge that can be trusted and produces confidence in the Way.

The Pali Canon mentions other kinds of faith as well. Faith through attainment (*agamaniya saddha*) is the abiding confidence in the merit of good deeds and of the Triple Gem which develops after receiving recognition and assurance of future Buddhahood. Faith through realization and understanding (*adhigama saddha*), on the other hand, is the confidence acquired through having won the fruits of the path i.e., knowledge and experience of nirvana. Faith by conviction (*okappana saddha*) is an unshakable faith and confidence inspired by the noble attributes of the Buddha, the Dharma, and the Sangha.

Reflecting this multi-dimensional aspect of faith, a great many Zen terms which designate practices involving faith are, quite understandably, interchangeable or concomitant. Take *shinko*, for example, the Japanese word most often translated as belief, creed, or faith. This term is usually equated with *shinpo* or belief. Both terms can be expressed in English by such words as faith, belief, devotion, commitment, and religious sentiment. Another word, *shojin*, is almost interchangeable with *shinjin*, meaning devotion or diligence.[26]

---

26. Borup, *Japanese Rinzai Zen Buddhism*, 125.

The Pali term usually translated as faith, saddha (Sanskrit: *sraddha*), also has multiple meanings. The verbal root of saddha is *sath* which means to be trustful, steadfast, confident, and to have conviction. The suffix *dha* means to support, uphold, and to sustain. Saddha is also described in Buddhist texts as a mental faculty, just as sight, hearing, smell, taste, and touch are faculties. It also might simply refer to anything or any act that is performed with sincerity and conviction. All these nuances have operated successfully within the Buddhist tradition.

Unfortunately, three things about the above have not often been recognized in the West. That is, the multi-faceted nature of faith, the treasure trove of varied faith activities, and the diversity of language surrounding them. So, while non-English terms relating to faith can demonstrate pliant boundaries and contextual flexibility, this is usually not clearly reflected in English. At times this has channeled our understanding of Zen faith into a dangerously reductive funnel.

For example, the Pali terms for faith (saddha), affection (*pema*) serene confidence, clarity, equanimity (pasada) and homage, veneration and devotion (*bhakti*) all convey different aspects of the meanings embodied in just one English term—devotion.[27] So our notions of what the above are, as well as the boundaries we in the West have drawn around them, are not as concrete or justified as they might first appear.

Even words related to faith which are not drawn from non-English sources have enabled many of us to box faith, consciously or unconsciously, into our own self-chosen corner. Belief, for example, is most equated with unfounded and unproven conjecture. For many of us belief carries negative pejorative meanings like faith when faith is seen as any cognitive content held to be true.

This Euro-centric view of faith sees belief as cognitive assent. In other words, a person consciously chooses to accept a doctrine as true. In this perspective, "I believe in" and "I have faith in" are synonymous, and belief is drawn in contrast to knowledge. It is a closed system which does not allow for flexibility but instead is built on a fixed set of propositional truth claims.

However, belief can simply mean a systemic collection of practices and doctrine such as those outlined in chapter 3 *The Path to Enlightenment: Buddhist Beliefs* in Jack Maguire's *Essential Buddhism: A Complete Guide to Beliefs and Practices*. Like faith, belief may also mean a state of mind in which trust or conviction is placed in something, whether that be a teacher

27. See Karunaratna, "Devotion," 435.

or the Triple Gem. It seems beliefs about belief can be just as diverse as they are about faith.

If we have the first interpretation of belief, however, then my reaction to the word faith may be representative of other Zen practitioners in the West. When I first encountered the word in a Zen context, I could not reconcile it with what I had heard about the rationality of Buddhism. In an intellectual quandary, I scrabbled around in my educational and religious knowledge to reconcile the two.

As a Study of Religion teacher with a degree in the Sociology of Religion, I settled on Martin Southwold's distinction between "believing that" (belief) and "believing in" (faith as trust). Southwold is from the University of Manchester, so I reckoned that this was an informed and useful distinction. In due course, however, this was superseded by an anthropological definition by the late Roy Rappaport in which he made a distinction between belief and acceptance, the former being akin to faith in something which arises out of personal experience. This, too, did not last. Hence, this book. It came out of a strong desire to understand just what Zen faith is.

Unfortunately, this task has been made unnecessarily difficult by the imbalanced aftermath of condescending colonial-era authors whose categorizations of Buddhist faith were limited to patronizing descriptions of a form of mysticism or a kind of primitive religious devotion employed by lay people who have false confidence in divine forces.[28]

A glaring example of bias and/or misrepresentation comes from the Reverend David Bowman Schneder, a Christian missionary to Japan. In his 1899 book *Japanese Buddhism* he condescended to write the following about Japanese Pure Land:

> This was the first Buddhist sect to announce the doctrine of paradise, or heaven, and of salvation by faith, though it did so in *a negative way*. Owing to a conviction that men were no longer as earnest in matters of religion as formerly, and that this few would attain to Nirvana according to the noble eight-fold path of original Buddhism, it was decided *to lower the standard*, and to find, *not "a more excellent,"* but an easier way [my italics].[29]

Lower the standard? If his intention was to pitch the Pure Land tradition within a negative framework for a Western audience, he succeeded.

28. Scott, "Hindu and Christian Bhakti," 12.

29. Scheder, *Japanese Buddhism*, 16.

Just recently I was given a copy of *Exploring Buddhism* by the respected and well-known Buddhist apologist Christmas Humphries. Humphries mentions faith 16 times, almost always in the negative. He writes that Buddhists come to realization not through dogma or with the help of faith, but checkable, usable, cold fact. He states that in the end "mere faith" is transformed into true knowledge. Buddhism doesn't need faith, Humphries claims, since religious faith and devotion, being "merely the first steps" on the Path, are themselves not enough.

These sorts of statements and the tone employed by them are constant reminders that in the West faith has (and continues to be) viewed within a conditional framework—as either blind belief or "just" a limited, preliminary stage of practice.

Other Buddhologists from last century such as Edward Conze also employed this trope. He stated (somewhat unkindly) in a chapter entitled *The Buddhism of Faith and Devotion* in his book *Buddhism: Its Essence and Development* that devotional faith is for those laymen and women who, being "incapable of wisdom, must use faith."

Rather than expressing the fact that equally valid but different paths to the Way cater to different abilities and personalities, Conze took a narrow and reductive view—that faith is always a "rather subordinate virtue" suitable only for those who favor theistic forms of religious expression. Many other important and respected teachers and scholars have also unquestionably assumed a similar and automatic concordance not only between faith and devotional forms of practice, but between devotion and blind faith.

Despite the ubiquitous nature of these perceptions, however, the fact is that faith does not always occur within the confines of just devotional forms of practice, and neither is it always blind. This misconception, at least in the West, seems to be another consequence of twentieth-century scholars once again arbitrarily dividing Buddhism into exclusive categories. In this case, the division of devotion (faith) and *magga* or the path.

Another consequence of this historical narrative is that some of us have taken Walpola Rahula's statement that "faith, as understood by most religions, has little to do with Buddhism" as completely axiomatic for all types of faith. Rahula, an eminent monk, scholar, and writer, saw faith as submission to a deity. He did not include other definitions in his assessment which meant that he also contrasted faith and knowledge.

The former, he suggested, is employed by "popular" Buddhism through faith-based devotion to the Triple Gem, while the true follower of Buddhism avoids this. (I wonder what he would've said to the late Zen Master Sheng-Yen who declared in his book *Orthodox Chinese Buddhism* that having faith in the Three Jewels is the most characteristic feature of a Buddhist.) Disapproval and distaste can clearly be seen in Rahula's statements, as well as a one-dimensional view of devotional practices.

It does demonstrate, of course, the tendency of modern human beings to create oppositional dichotomies. Many of us like to divide things into fixed categories which separate the world into absolutes such as love and hate, virtue and vice, death and life, men and women, and praise and condemnation.

In terms of a discussion of faith, this means that we divide religion from Zen, religion from science, the rational from the irrational, and experience from the magical. As I have suggested previously, it is common in the West to see the path of faith as one thing and reason another. These two categories are often pitched as mutually exclusive. A Google search easily reveals a plethora of materials supporting such a view.

They are typical of the kind of unchallenged and almost automatic categorical divisions often made in the West and illustrate the fact that over-generalized and mutually exclusive views of faith and reason are the natural go-to for many of us. Thanissaro Bhikkhu was right when he said that many Westerners play fast and loose with the Buddhist notion of faith.

5

Faith Re-Imagined

In the previous chapter I mentioned that adapting the practice to our own situation is an entirely reasonable thing to do. It becomes less so, however, if in doing so we lose sight of the relational and interdependent nature of things and judge them instead by where they lie on a continuum between polar opposites which are falsely held to be objective realities. This runs contrary to the Middle Way, which avoids clinging to opposites through the direct realization of the essential unity of all things. If we do not take flexible approaches to faith, therefore, we may not be able to bypass the tendency to polarize into one thing or the other.

Let's explore this notion further. In the West there is a historical tendency to separate religion from philosophy. The problem with this oppositional dichotomy is that it runs contrary to historical fact in the East—that religion and philosophy have almost always been inseparable. To disconnect these ignores the fact that Buddhism has never known the West's great divide between faith and reason, and religion and philosophy. In fact, the latter two have been described by Buddhists as two forks of the same tree. Both stem from the same roots and are nourished by the same sap.

In addition, by not examining our own perceptions about these categories we ironically exclude the faith most mentioned in both Theravada and Mahayana sutras—faith as a kind of working hypothesis in the Dharma—the very kind of scientific, rationalist tendency that attracted many Westerners to Buddhism in the first place.

If we take a purely oppositional stance, then, flexible lateral shifts may not be apparent to us or even considered. We can totally pass over the established historical fact that Zen has engaged in a variety of legitimate methods and experiences, including faith. This is unjust to faith because it ignores its many facets and reduces it to a matter of epistemology, that is, faith is seen purely through the lens of *what do you know?* This confines faith to a narrow definition and does not do it justice nor approach it holistically.

Of course, this is not to say that knowability is unimportant. Rather, that in concentrating on it to the detriment of other aspects, we inadvertently box faith into a framework which fails to address the topic in a comprehensive, reasonable manner. In assuming that the categories of current western epistemology are uniformly adequate for interpreting all spiritual approaches, we prejudge faith and confine it to a particular bandwidth which tends to rule out or downplay legitimate affective methods.

Moreover, when we make the determination to see faith through narrow lenses, we risk stereotyping people and their practices, the very problem some of us might have with the black and white thinking of faith-based theism. It is to the detriment of Zen in the West, therefore, that at times it has not recognized that its own black and white thinking has permitted little flexibility.

A more panoramic view allows us to find alternatives. Instead of automatically assuming that the alternative to rationality (represented by pure Buddhism) is irrationality (represented by faith) we might take a step sideways. We can, for example, consider what both philosopher Ken Wilder and Vipassana teacher Mary Jo Meadow call the trans-rational—the stages of development which have to do with awareness and the number of perspectives one can encompass.

The trans-rational approach sees Zen as an interior kind of science which draws from all manner of methods to confirm judgment. It steps outside of categories and does not privilege Western epistemological frameworks in the assessment of religious knowledge over non-Western and/or non-rationalist ones. A trans-rational approach recognizes that Zen is not fixed. It is flexible enough to use the entire range of our mental, emotional, intellectual, and spiritual abilities.

That includes emotion. Some Western Zen practitioners have a degree of discomfort over what they perceive as a by-product of faith, that is, the negative or exclusionary link faith engenders between emotion and reason.

As I mentioned previously, emotion is often automatically paired with irrationality and/or methods of blind faith. Faith is then incorrectly summed up as either an untrustworthy method or a kind of unfounded devotionalism. This is certainly not the case.

It is important, then, that at some point we step back and wait till the smoke clears. We may then note that either/or statements do us no favor. In terms of emotion and reason, we can see that while faith in Zen is not separate from emotion, it is, at the same time, not dependent on it. As we explore in the next two chapters, Zen has always involved the affective dimension.

Furthermore, there is a qualitative difference between having emotions and being dominated by them. We need to recognize that any discussion of faith cannot help but include emotions, especially positive and profitable feelings of serenity, lucidity, and equanimity because these arise as a matter of course in well-conducted practice. If Buddhism frowned upon emotion in favor of reason alone, it would've been impossible for it to flourish as it has.

The point, then, is that we need to ask ourselves whether common perceptions and distinctions are really so set in stone. Can we realistically draw a distinct line between the workings of "faith" and Zen "experience" for example? After all, in placing our faith in the practice, lineage, the teacher and Zen itself, aren't we somehow paying tribute to the fact that realization can only be addressed through a degree of emotional commitment?

For the Zen practitioner, faith must demand some kind of affective conviction. To sit in the trust and hope that Zen is not lying to us implies that it is not a dry intellectual affair. In fact, to overly concentrate on intellect and ignore other affective aspects has been described by some Zen masters as "dried up Zen."

In his Shobogenzo (Treasure of the True Dharma Eye), Dogen stated that it is the *kokoro* that truly trusts; it is the body of true faith. Since Buddhists have traditionally considered emotion and intellect to be virtually inseparable, the Japanese word which Dogen used is more accurately rendered as heart-mind. Faith, therefore, is a matter of wholeness. It does not isolate emotion from wisdom or intellect as long as is within a balanced, holistic framework.

This means that Buddhist experience is in no way antithetical to Western thinking nor is it anti-rational. As such, we can certainly grasp the essence of key concepts such as *sunyata* (emptiness) through logical reason. The difference from a purely logical approach is that Buddhism also requires us to combine this with faithful practice since the intellectual concept of sunyata must be deepened through clarity and concentration which are preconditions for the unclouded function of the logical power of understanding.[1]

Soma Thera further explains:

> There are some people who, without examining the Dhamma properly, speak of it as a kind of rationalism, and of the Buddha as an early rationalist . . . By such talk they cause a good deal of misunderstanding. There is no doubt that the Buddha was rational and that his teaching accords with reason. But it is incorrect to call him a rationalist. He was one of robust faith. His faith was connected with knowledge and founded on it. It is because the Bodhisatta had faith in truth and his ability to find it that he went forth from home to homelessness. He was of an analytical turn of mind from the very start of his quest . . . But for applying what he found out by analysis to life he required faith, and he saw that it was indispensable in his experiments with aspects of the truth he reached as a seeker. It was his faith that carried him from partial understanding ever onward.[2]

Thera is pointing out that Buddhist faith is not entirely rationalistic but that this does not automatically necessitate moving to the extreme ends of our continuum of opposites and assume the Way is irrational. Instead, we can find balance.

To do this successfully, we must remind ourselves that the guiding purpose of the Dharma is liberation from suffering not the knowledge of facts. So, while the Dharma might be compatible with science to a large degree, the discovery of scientific data and logical proofs is not its aim. For this reason, it doesn't seek intellectual or categorical assent but full spiritual emancipation. It asks for a response which is holistic.

A holistic response awakens faith, devotion, and commitment as appropriate methods by which to seek liberation since they impel us to enter and persevere along the path. If we see the function of faith in light of the purpose of the Dharma, then we see that it serves the same function as critical inquiry—liberation. There are not two faces of the Dharma but one.

1. Bruck and Lai, *Buddhismus und Christentum*, 55.
2. Thera, "Faith in the Buddha's Teachings," 5–22, 7–8.

Consequently, we sell Buddhist faith short if we perceive it as a purely emotional, non-reasoned act exclusive of wisdom and which is always directed at a deity. This is viewing it through a narrow tunnel because faith in Buddhism is comprehensive—it includes emotion and devotion so long as they are within a particular and deliberate framework. After all, even too much faith or trust in the wise authority of a realized person is still blind faith, and any attachment, even to a buddha, is a hindrance to realization.

Both Zen and Theravada Buddhisms hold that since faith is detrimental if carried to excess it must be restrained and supported by wisdom both mundane and supra-mundane. Likewise, dry intellect must be flavored with faith to obtain satisfactory results. The Visuddhimagga (The Path of Purification), a comprehensive manual condensing and systematizing the early theoretical and practical teachings of the Buddha, commented on the need for a proper balance between faith and knowledge.

Its author, Buddhaghosa, taught that if we are strong in faith but weak in understanding, our confidence tends to lack critical clarity and is groundless. If, however, we have a strong understanding but are weak in faith, we tend to err on the side of cunning and can be hard to cure of our self-interest. It often leads to cleverness and a superficially critical way of evaluating things. Both hinder spiritual progress. With the balancing of wisdom and faith, however, a person has confidence only when there are grounds for it.

In fact, faith and wisdom are the two wings upon which realization depends. The Samyutta Nikaya (The Connected Discourses of the Buddha) points out that faith and wisdom are forever yoked together. This is why faith without its partner, wisdom, leads to imbalance. This is echoed in the words of the great master Zhiyi, the fourth ancestor of Tiantai Buddhism, who also claimed that both are essential for a correct understanding of the teachings.

> If wisdom and faith are both present then when one hears that any single instant of thought is itself the right [thought of enlightenment], one's faith will prevent one from disparaging [this teaching], while one's wisdom will prevent one from fearing it. In this case the beginning and the end will both be right. But if one lacks faith, one will think of the saintly realms as so lofty and far-removed that one has no stake in their wisdom, while if one lacks wisdom, one will become exceedingly arrogant, declaring oneself

> to be equal of the Buddha. Under such circumstances, beginning
> and end will both be in error.[3]

Thus, a person "who has understanding, establishes his faith in accordance with that understanding." In this way, the Samyutta Nikaya (The Connected Discourses of the Buddha) tells us, faith becomes a friend of humanity when it is controlled by wisdom because balance between the elements of the Way facilitates effective practice. Thus, "the wise, seeing their own welfare, gain faith in enlightenment, the teaching, and community."

So, faith and wisdom are two terms which describe the same kind of motivation, just seen from two different perspectives. If we look closely, we realize that faith is a capacity to see the truth. Faith and wisdom are together one form of intelligence that discerns between what is wholesome, skillful and what is harmful and dangerous.[4]

If we take note of what the Buddha said in the Pali Canon as a conclusion to the well-known Kalama Sutta, we see that he asked the Kalamas to go on faith which is grounded in their own heartfelt wisdom and experience.

> But when you know *for yourselves* that certain teachings are not
> good, that when you put them into practice they lead to loss and
> suffering, you must then *trust* yourselves and reject them. [my
> italics]

The Buddha was talking about *akaravanti saddha* or what early Buddhists called justified faith. This refers to the development and realization of faith in perfect wisdom (prajna) via trusting confidence, resoluteness, deliberation, weighing up and testing. In the Majjhima Nikaya (The Middle-length Discourses) the Buddha stated that a person's faith should be reasoned and rooted in understanding and that they are tasked with investigating and testing the object of their faith.

Buddhist faith is not in conflict with the spirit of inquiry, and to have doubt about dubitable things is completely acceptable because it leads to realization. Part of faith is to question, to seek understanding and the wisdom of learning. So justified faith in a Buddhist context refers to a reasonable, warranted type of knowing. It does not refer to a purely empirical, logical, or philosophical line of reasoning, though these can play a part.

In no way, then, is akaravanti saddha blind faith. It is informed faith manifested in entrustment of one's own experiential wisdom. This is what

---

3. See Pap, "Faith in Zhanran's Diamond Scalpel Treatise," 50–51.

4. Giustarinin, "Faith and Renunciation in Early Buddhism," 166, 175, 177.

the Buddha asked the Kalamas to do—to form working hypotheses by taking what wise people value and then testing those hypotheses to find a workable outcome.

This is also what Zen adherents do when they take up Zen—they take it on faith that the Buddha and all the ancestors of Zen were telling the truth about realization. In an interview about Zen practice, my teacher, Seiun An Roshi, was once asked, "What is faith, from the Buddhist perspective?" She answered, "Faith that the practice works and faith that I can realize—that realization is not reserved for some special elect."[5]

In other words, to practice Zen is to practice in the faith that realization is really and truly possible. It is to confirm for ourselves what the Zen ancestors taught. To neglect or minimize this aspect, therefore, is to selectively marginalize a useful and legitimate element of the Way.

There is an important caveat to this, however. Zen has always wisely recognized that different kinds of faith utilize different affective aspects and that these serve an array of useful purposes as long as a certain stipulation is applied. That is, it must be recognized that proper practice doesn't just stop at faith's development, it must also involve discernment about the type of faith we develop, since not all are profitable.

In fact, right from the start of Buddhism, both baseless faith (i.e., blind, irrational, rootless or uncritical faith) such as that shown by Brahmins in the Canki Sutta (they declared that only the Vedic hymn *Mantapada* was true and all others were false) and professed faith were discouraged by the Buddha. Baseless faith is in direct contrast to faith with a good cause, faith founded on seeing and wise faith. Professed faith is an outward or seeming faith which is channeled into empty performance and appearances rather than the development of wisdom.

The Mahaparinibbana Sutta (Buddha's Last Days) shows us certain times in which even Ananda, the Buddha's cousin, and disciple, enacted an unprofitable and overly intense faith. In a discussion at the Capala Shrine, Ananda's faith prevented rather than enhanced appreciation of the Buddha's words. Even though the Buddha considered Ananda an exceptional attendant, sometimes his faith was too other-oriented and overly affective. Faith didn't entirely work for Ananda because it was directed towards the Buddha as a person. This meant that he was sometimes too attached and his faith too emotional to discern the wisdom of his own cousin's words.

5. Sweeping Zen, "Sei'un An Roselyn Stone Interview," 1.

Ananda's kind of faith is known as pema, strong affection. It can be a positive thing when accompanied by insight, respect, and self-control. Vasubandhu's Abhidharmakosa-bhasya (Verses on the Treasury of Abhidharma) is representative of the Mahayana view of pema—that a discerning person who reflects on the threefold perfection of the Buddha cannot help but develop profound affection. The Theragatha (Verses of the Elder Monks) of the Theravada Pali Canon states that whoever knows their teacher's teachings should firmly dwell in them and produce affection.

Yet pema can be a fetter when it manifests as solicitousness, extreme zealousness, and overly intense devotion. So, although a reverential and devotional attitude of mind is the natural outcome of true understanding, the Buddha discouraged excessive veneration paid to him personally. Intense faith directed towards powerful personalities rather than the Dharma is misdirected faith whereas the proper understanding and use of faith avoids the downside of unhealthy affection and overly emotional faith. Used correctly, then, faith aids our transformation and development; used incorrectly, it is nothing but a hindrance.

Bhakti is a good illustrative example of this. In its original Hindu context, it refers to the devotion and the love of a personal god or a representational god by a devotee. It means to become part of and involves the practice of surrendering to and unification with a transcendent deity.

Up until recently it was common for modern Buddhists to unquestioningly assume that this theistic bhakti was synonymous with devotion in Buddhism. Even as late as 1992, we can find clear examples of this type of thinking:

> As Mahayana Buddhism developed, the concept of God, *Buddha as God* began to take place. The tradition of *worship* gradually increased . . . after the demise of Buddha, slowly and slowly his image was adorned by his followers. The major and minor disciples accepted him as the *supreme God*. Thus devotion or bhakti emerged in Mahayana Buddhism. He was called Amitabha Buddha [my italics].[6]

This interpretation involves certain fundamental errors of perception outlined by the Buddha, first and foremost, that devotion involves the worship of a deity or God-Buddha. This is counter to the Buddha's teachings of dependent arising. Moreover, it does not call for examination and release of the ego-self, but for an encounter with a supreme entity—to participate in

---

6. Sekido, "Bhakti and Sraddha," 984–993.

God and internalize God. When meant in this sense, it is entirely correct to say that bhakti is not the doctrine of Buddhism.

When meant in a non-theistic sense, however, devotion is legitimately part and parcel of the Zen Way. This is because Zen practice rests on the objective fact that we are already the transcendent truth. Faith-based practices such as Pure Land also rest on this fact since on an essential level there is nothing to be unified with because Amida Buddha (the buddha who is the focus of devotion in Pure Land) is not a higher being as such. Amida represents infinite time and space and neither comes from any place nor goes anywhere else. As a result, he is not an ontological other or something higher than the mind of the practitioner because both a person's mind of faith and the mind of Amida are non-dual.

This means that the faith of faith-based Buddhism is not the same as the kind of faith seen in Christianity. Even when Christian mystics talk of union with God, it is, by their own definition, not an experience of complete interdependence and interpenetration. This is because while self and God are closely intertwined and connected, a separation between them is always maintained.

On the surface Pure Land faith might appear to be the same as this because its faith is none other than the true and real mind of Amida Buddha operating in us, but this is not so. While it is true that Amida facilitates realization in the mind of the individual, there is a difference in what the practitioner realizes. This is not the true nature of a being outside or apart from us, but rather the true nature of all reality, oneself included. Thus, as a person engages in the practices of Pure Land faith—recitation and visualization—they come to a deeper realization of their true existence, and the non-duality between themselves and Amida.[7]

Devotional or otherwise, therefore, Zen expressions of faith are essentially different from Hindu bhakti and Christian union. Faith in Amida does have some elements in common with devotion in both of these religions, but it's worth noting that the term bhakti does not even appear in the Sukhavativyuha Sutra (Infinite Life Sutra), the main text of the Pure Land sect.[8] In fact, none of the words which represent different types of faith in Buddhism mean the kind of absolute belief in and devotion to an absolute person indicated by the Hindu term bhakti.

7. Largen, "Appreciation and Appropriation," 112.

8. Hirakawa, *A History of Indian Buddhism from Sakyamuni to Early Mahayana*, 290.

In Buddhist faith, then, there is no element of a purely emotional affection or blind credulity. Since nothing is separate in the first place, neither has it ever involved any separate entity uniting with another. The Yuzu Nembutsu Shu (Interfusing Pure Land School), for example, would most certainly take issue with anyone who claimed this since its entire doctrine is based on interfusion—the fact that all people and things are mutually related and interdependent. In Pure Land terms, this means that our own recitation of the nembutsu influences all others and vice versa, interacting to help bring about the rebirth of all in the Pure Land.

Jichihan (Jippan), one of the earliest figures to interpret Pure Land ideas from an esoteric standpoint, is another example of Mahayana non-dualism. In his mind-only Pure Land practice he taught that since there is no discrimination in the single dharma realm, Buddha's pure land is also our mind. This means that the person who contemplates and the object of contemplation (in this case, Amida Buddha), as well as the person who achieves birth and the place where they are born, are in no way separate at all.

This echoes Keiji Nishitani's observation about Zen:

> Zen does not wish to recognize, as the resting place of the investigation into self, some transcendent being, to the extent that this would be thought as an 'Other' to the self which stands in front of the self, opposed to the self, outside of the self . . . Zen rejects the view that the final place arrived at is that of absolute devotion, faith, and worship to—or gratitude for the grace received from— such an absolute 'Other'.[9]

Devotional faith aspects of Buddhist practice should not, therefore, be equated with those of theistic faith nor automatically dismissed as irrational and contrary to dependent origination since enlightened faith is based on the truth of non-duality.

As Nyanaponika Thera correctly notes for both Theravada and Mahayana practice:

> . . . it would be a mistake to conclude that the Buddha disparaged a reverential and devotional attitude of mind when it is the natural outflow of a true understanding and a deep admiration of what is great and noble. It would also be a grievous error to believe that the "seeing of the Dhamma" . . . is identical with a mere intellectual appreciation and purely conceptual grasp of the doctrine. Such a

9. Nishitani, *Collected Works of Nishitani Keiji*, 214.

one-sided abstract approach to the very concrete message of the Buddha all too often leads to intellectual smugness.

> Devotion, being a facet and natural accompaniment of confidence, is a necessary factor in the "balance of faculties" required for final deliverance. Confidence, in all its aspects, including the devotional, is needed to resolve any stagnation and other shortcomings resulting from a one-sided development of the intellectual faculties. Such development often tends to turn around in circles endlessly, without being able to effect a break-through. Here, devotion, confidence and faith—all aspects of the Pali term *saddha*—may be able to give quick and effective help.[10]

On the balance of the available facts, then, I would like to put forward the notion that the sheer number and variety of these faith practices suggest that a full and proper accounting of Zen faith cannot help but involve acknowledging cognitive, conative, and affective aspects if we are to create understandings which are comprehensively faithful and true to the Buddha Dharma.

Cognitive aspects of faith relate to intellectual understanding, thought, or knowledge based on doctrines or teachings as well as experiential investigation and testing. Conative relates to such things as vows, the will, determination, and energy. This is important for Zen practitioners, for example, since it is the opposite of, or an antidote against, the sluggishness, dejection, and discouragement that can arise during long hours of meditation practice.[11] Lastly, the affective aspect refers to sincere appreciation and satisfaction for the teaching and the teacher, as well as trust and reliance.

Given the widespread and almost automatic correlation between faith, devotion and non-rational or theistic inclinations, however, it is no surprise that bhakti (in its Hindu sense) is still sometimes used disparagingly to describe *any* Buddhist faith practice. Consequently, faith in whatever form it takes is still seen in some circles as ineffective and improper for a Buddhist.

Nevertheless, there it stands, a constant presence throughout the centuries of Buddhist practice. As the Buddha himself often stated, all who go for refuge to him, the teaching, and the community, do so "out of faith." As *Tricycle: The Buddhist Review* correctly notes in its *Buddhism for Beginners Level 1* section entitled *Is faith important in Buddhism*:

10. Thera, *Devotion in Buddhism: Three Essays*, 7.

11. Gomez, "Faith," 278.

A common perception in the modern West is that faith departs from Buddhism's core concerns. But throughout its history, faith has played an essential role in bringing the dharma to life.[12]

Sao Pannyanada sums it up well:

> . . . it is generally believed that there is no place for faith in Buddhism. It has been argued that Buddhism is a non-theistic religion and therefore there is no savior in whom one should have faith. In addition, it is pointed out that Buddhism considers one to be one's own master and therefore it is not faith that is important but effort. Yet it is clearly seen that in the early Buddhist scriptures themselves there are numerous references which show that some kind of faith plays an important role in Buddhism. Taking refuge in the Buddha, Dhamma and Sangha shows that there must be some form of faith in the act of taking refuge. Correspondingly, numerous terms are used which convey some idea of faith.[13]

The late Soto master, the Very Reverend Keido Chisan Koho Zenji, former Abbot of Sojiji, confirmed this for Zen as well.

He pointed out that in Zen it is generally believed that the doctrine of faith is something limited to the Pure Land School. Yet faith in the original vow of the Buddha as taught by Shinran, invocation of the Lotus Sutra taught by Nichiren, realization of one's innate enlightenment as taught by Dogen, are all examples of teachings based on faith.[14]

Koho also taught that it is no exaggeration to say that the peace of mind which is the object of the Soto Zen school is impossible without faith. Zen transmission, he pointed out, is not based on historical studies, but stands firmly on deep faith. The way to dispel illusion, therefore, can only be found with the help of correct faith. Koho considered this the only way to arrive at selflessness.[15]

No doubt he took inspiration from Dogen. As Francis Dojun Cook, author of *How to Raise an Ox: Zen Practice as Taught in Master Dogen's Shobogenzo* asserts:

> Dogen's Zen is the Zen of faith. That is, it is a religion in which faith is the very mechanism whereby the goal is achieved, and in the absence of which the door to the truth remains closed. It is

12. Tricycle.org, "Is Faith Important in Buddhism?," para. 5.
13. Pannyanada, "Saddha (Faith) is the Fundamental Step," para. 1.
14. Koho, *Soto Zen: An Introduction*, 72.
15. Koho, *Soto Zen: An Introduction*, 68, 72–73.

therefore not simply one important element among others; it is the indispensable prerequisite.[16]

Similarly, Xuyun, a renowned Chinese Zen master and one of the most influential Buddhist teachers of the 19th and 20th centuries, taught that a firm believing mind is the fundamental basis of training because faith is the mother or begetter of the beginning (the source) of right doctrine, and because without faith, "no good will derive therefrom."

Rinzai Zen teachers such as Nyogen Senzaki, for example, have also held a similar stance. Senzaki, one of the twentieth century's leading proponents of Rinzai Zen in the United States, stated that unless we have faith in being enlightened in this life, we had better not study Zen at all.

The late Sheng-Yen, a 57th generational dharma heir in the Rinzai tradition, maintained the position that without faith, one has not even entered the gate of Buddhist practice. In his opinion, since the Dharma is transmitted by a Zen master, if we don't first believe that we can practice it, there's no way they can transmit it to us.

In *Attaining the Way: A Guide to the Practice of Chan Buddhism* he outlines what he considers the bottom line for realization—that "without faith, a person cannot stand." He points out that without faith in the Buddha, there is no Dharma to learn, and without faith in the Sangha, we cannot be taught the Dharma. If we wish to enter the realm of Zen, he cautions, we must have complete faith in the Buddha, Dharma, and Sangha.[17]

For these Zen masters, therefore, faith is *the* (if not *an*) essential requirement to Zen practice and it is not until we have deep earnest faith that we will be able to attain and practice the Dharma. Whether we like it or not, then, faith has always been an integral part of Zen. In fact, in the Mahayana tradition a lack of faith has often been cited as one of the biggest hindrances to realization.

It is this aspect of Zen which most resembles Theravada principles in that faith is regarded by both traditions as "the seed," and without it, the plant of spiritual life cannot start at all. As the kernel of all wholesome states, it inspires the mind with confidence and determination to cross the flood of samsara. Without faith, we are unable to develop energy on the spiritual path and to enjoy the benefits of faith, that is, the ability to sustain

16. Cook, *How to Raise an Ox*, 129.
17. Sheng-Yen, *Attaining the Way*, 135.

confidence, remain steadfast, and embody a supporting trust, in the sense of abiding firmly.[18]

A re-examination of Zen faith can also allow us to become aware of the ways in which certain Euro and theistic outlooks might color our basic understandings of Zen, and the extent to which we are influenced by Western paradigms which separate faith and knowledge. In terms of God-centric outlooks, there are ample examples of Buddhism and Zen described in Christian terms such as theology, worship, eschatology, salvation, and even sin. These sorts of words can present a problem when Western assumptions become dominated by implicit Christian meanings which do not apply.

This notion of caution around the usage of Christian terms is certainly not new. Writing in 1953 in the respected journal *Light of the Dhamma*, Mauno Nordberg went so far as to say that it is "absolutely indispensable" to give up words like religion, sin, worship, salvation, and the like, when writing or speaking to Western audiences about the Dharma. He felt that this applied to any Western language.[19]

Unlike Nordberg, however, I do not suggest blanket prohibitions but a clearer understanding. Mu Soeng, author of *Trust in Mind: The Rebellion of Chinese Zen*, a recent book about the Xinxin Ming (Verses on the Faith in Mind), explains that he chose the word trust rather than faith in the title to "avoid the otherwise inevitable difficulties of context in a Judeo-Christian understanding."[20] While I sympathize, I believe that it is not always wise to avoid something because it might be misconstrued, especially if we can clarify its meaning.

If we can learn the complexities of terms such as one mind, non-abiding, shikantaza or buddha nature we can certainly manage faith. In this respect, I am with Sharon Salzberg, co-founder of the Insight Meditation Center, whose own motivation for writing a book about faith was to reclaim it for modern Buddhists and to open a discussion about its many facets.

> I want to encourage delight in the word, to help reclaim faith as fresh, vibrant, intelligent and liberating. This is a faith that emphasizes love and respect for ourselves as a foundation. It is a faith that uncovers our connection to others, rather than designating anyone as separate and apart.[21]

18. Park, *Buddhist Faith and Sudden Enlightenment*, 64.

19. *Nordberg*, "Is *Dhamma* a Religion?," 40–41.

20. Soeng, *Trust in Mind: The Rebellion of Chinese Zen*, 73.

21. Salzberg, *Faith: Trusting Your Own Deepest Experience*, xiv.

The beauty and utility of faith is that it is an inclusive word. Less encompassing terms such as confidence or trust do not capture the entire range of faith modalities and present a limited vision of its multi-faceted nature and role. Faith nicely encapsulates most alternate or associated words within this term.

So, while it is true that the English word faith has implications that can differ from its equivalents in Asian languages, such as sraddha (Sanskrit), saddha (Pali), *dad-pa* (Tibetan), *bisirel* (Mongolian), *xin* (Chinese), *sin* (Korean) and *shin* (Japanese), I take the position represented by Professor Luis O. Gomez. That is, with proper attention to contexts and the awareness of cultural differences, faith can be effectively used as a descriptive, analytical, or comparative tool in the understanding of Buddhist ideas and practices.[22]

If we use terms which are misunderstood or ambiguous in meaning and which might be inextricably bound up with other religions, we can make clear in what way we are using them. It is not a huge stretch of the imagination to anticipate that Western Zen Buddhists can come to a more precise definition of faith in Zen. It just requires accuracy, clarity, and a willingness to approach the West's faith hangover.

Moreover, a dialogue about the role and meaning of faith within Zen is also not only timely and pragmatic but a truly useful conduit by which to engage with traditions outside of Zen. It is not enough to just dismiss other traditions on the basis that they are "faith-based" because aspects of Zen practice are also based on faith. It too is faith-based.

In his article entitled *Tunnel Vision: The Surprise of Devotion in Zen*, the late Reverend Master Daizui MacPhillamy of the Order of Buddhist Contemplatives describes how his understanding of faith-practices progressed from the surprise that they actually existed in Zen to a warm appreciation that they did.

Mcphillamy witnessed ample positive results of faith-inclusive practices. He stated:

> We, who go into Zen feeling all stern and rigorous and alone and
> intellectually uncompromising, get sort of "mushied up" by it
> somewhere along the line. Hearts begin to open, minds begin to
> soften, eyes begin to twinkle with a touch of mischief, and we get
> bowled over by the sheer love and divinity of the universe, within
> which we still don't necessarily find anything that we'd want to call

22. Gomez, "Faith," 277.

"God." In other words, while the practices of Zen are generally not devotional, their consequences are.

> It is fascinating to see how this devotional side shows itself among old Zen monks and other long-term Zen students. They seem to just start finding time to paint, write music or poetry, arrange flowers, cook, make tea, celebrate ceremonies and generally do things that express their love for the whole world all of it in a spirit of joyful offering. In fact, they start acting as though their entire life was a series of offerings. It is here then, in the ceremonial, in the Zen arts, and in a thousand little unprompted acts of love, that one sees our devotional side. However, since our devotion is a spontaneous blossoming forth . . . it is easy to miss.[23]

Even in our seemingly non-devotional Zen, there are practices which many would classify as "devotional"—vows, bowing, the offering of food and incense, and the chanting of verses dedicated to various bodhisattvas. The line drawn between various traditions may seem definitive, but it often suits polemic more than reality.

Take, for example, the modern re-discovery by well-known and respected teachers at several US Zen centers of the benefit of sewing Zen robes, a devotional act which has had a long tradition in Zen, particularly in the Soto sect. In Zen sewing Buddha's Robe is a practice for both the laity and priests and is based upon the rice paddy pattern of the Buddha's own robes which he made from scraps of material. Most garments worn by monks and nuns of all schools are sewn together in this traditional design.

Zen's high level of regard for the *kasyapa* (robe) is reflected in the fact that it is used as a synonym for emptiness itself. Dogen, for example, compared the act of putting on the kasyapa "the same as when a prince ascends the throne." In fact, he taught that the robe is itself the very body of Buddha; that it is not other than zazen.

This high level of respect and gratitude for the virtue of not only sewing the robe but the robe itself, clearly emanate from the many descriptive titles it has been given—the clothing of emancipation, the robe of the field of benefaction, the robe beyond form, the robe of patience, the Tathagata's robe, the robe of great love and great compassion, the robe as a victorious banner, and the robe of unsurpassable, complete, enlightenment.[24] These describe both phenomenal and essential aspects of the robe.

23. MacPhillamy, "Tunnel Vision: The Surprise of Devotion in Zen," 1.

24. Sugawara, "Kesa Kudoku: Virtue of the Kashaya," 1.

So how does sewing practice supplement other Zen practices, express devotion or even enable realization in itself? How do these inter-relate and co-condition each other? In her book *The Role of Devotion in Sewing Buddha's Robe* Jean Selkirk, the primary sewing teacher at the Berkeley Zen Center, notes that devotion is the unseen tension and pattern weaving threads of practice into cloth. Turned into robes, she points out, devotion truly expresses heart-mind, the intersection of feeling and thought embodied. She describes precisely how the process of sewing robes becomes a devotional act.

> First, setting a mindful approach toward the chosen activity, similar to a short pause before bowing, or an offering itself, meant to gather our own and/or others's energy for the task. Second, the respectful energy continues into the activity. Third, maintaining intention while engaged in activities even without an objective. Intention may serve as the "object" usually associated with devotion that may also be a person, transcendent idea, feeling, or practice. Fourth, leaving nothing out, not the mind, not the heart, not the body, but bringing every part of oneself into the experience. Finally, continuing in a dedicated, faithful way: offering the merit without gaining mind.[25]

She suggests that, in the act of sewing, self and other-power meet (see chapter 8 for a further discussion of other-power). This is because devotion allows in the entire buddha field and ancestors as support, it acts as a conduit for the aspiration of "coming from within the real" and of the way-seeking mind connecting with inspiration, while all the time encouraging the potential of the formless field of benefaction.

Selkirk also notes that for many of her sewing students, the role of devotion in Zen is like a koan in that some of them are under the impression that Zen discourages reverence and veneration altogether. Not so, says Selkirk. Respect and reverence still have their place even in a Way without a deity. In the act of repeating the phrase *namu kie butsu* (I take Refuge in the Buddha) with every stitch, the act of sewing becomes a mantra and mindful practice in itself. That is, it returns to the self which is one with the universe and in doing so, enacts true co-creation.

The late and much respected Zenkei Blanche Hartman, former Abbot of the San Francisco Zen Center, and sewing teacher at SFZC agreed:

---

25. Selkirk, "The Role of Devotion in Sewing Buddha's Robe," para. 9.

> Sewing Buddha's Robe is first and foremost a devotional practice.
> Each sewing session begins by offering incense with three prostra-
> tions and each session ends with three bows. Taking refuge with
> each stitch immerses me in just this stitch, stitch after stitch, just
> as following the exhale immerses me in just this breath as I sit I
> sit zazen. Through each stitch we express faith, devotion and love
> through the medium of sewing.[26]

Thus, the real point of a devotional act in Zen is not unsubstantiated belief which occurs separately and/or without the experiential knowledge
of awakening. To sew robes is to become one with what we do because
it exemplifies and embodies the principle known in Japanese as *nyoho-e*.
Nyo means as-it-is-ness, as in showing the truth as it really is, *ho* the Law,
truth, or the Buddha's teaching, and *e* the robe. This is why the Saddharmapundarika Sutra (Lotus Sutra) states that the robe of the Tathagata is the
Buddha's flexible and forbearing mind; the kind of mind which opens to
everything.

Zen teacher Eijun Linda Cutts, Senior Teacher at the San Francisco
Zen Center, eloquently describes how this comes about:

> With a presence and clarity, and attention to detail, stitch after
> stitch after breath after vow after stitch after vow . . . and each stitch,
> each breath . . . is completely fresh, is completely unmanifested
> until stitch, stitch, breath . . . each stitch is almost the same and
> the earth bursts into flame with each moment . . . Each moment is
> right in the middle of the fullness of our life, the heat, the massive
> fire. It may seem, with our karmic life . . . with our conditioning,
> that the next moment is predetermined . . . But . . . our life . . . at
> each moment is completely, utterly, free.[27]

Tomoe Katagiri, a teacher with extensive experience in teaching robe-
making at the Minnesota Zen Meditation Center, emphasizes that to fully
understand the wearing of Buddha robes, a Zen practitioner must recognize its three aspects—its practical use as clothing, its ceremonial use as
a religious garment, and the act of receiving it as the Buddha's body and
mind.[28]

Again, the reason that sewing the robe can be both valid and profitable spiritually is precisely because it not a mere piece of cloth or just the

26. Hartman, "Foreword, "para. 3.

27. Cutts, "Sewing Buddha's Robe," 1.

28. Katagiri, *Study of the Okesda: Nyohoe The Buddha's Robe,* 3.

act of sewing. In a certain sense, its pattern might also be thought of as a mandala representing the world.

> Each Kesa is Buda's original Kesa. When we wear it, we are dressed by the cosmic order. It's the cosmic order which practices Zazen, and we ourselves are the cosmic order sitting in Zazen. The Kesa is material: it is composed of clothing and thread. It is also immaterial: the silent transmission from master to disciple.[29]

Clearly, robe sewing is a meditative *and* devotional Zen practice which unifies body, breath, and mind.

This is not limited to sewing robes, however, it can also occur via other traditional Zen practices such as sutra copying, recitation or chanting. Yasutani, for example, pointed out the practical results of chants and sutras in terms of faith—that the intoning of sutras is a mode of zazen. For those whose faith in the Way requires development, he noted, the repeated chanting of sutras eventually leads to a measure of understanding which serves to strengthen faith in the truth of the Buddha's teachings.

In Zen, sacred text is chanted or read in two main ways—searching for their meaning i.e., reaffirming the teaching and vowing to practice, or reading with *mushin*. Mushin literally means "the mind without mind" and is commonly called the state of no-mindedness. A non-abiding mind does not, however, refer to the absence of thought but of not being trapped in thoughts or not adhering to a certain conceptual habit or position. This state of pure mental clarity arises when the mind is fully present, aware, and free.

This means that, with the attitude of faith and the state of mushin, reading or chanting can have as much value as meditation. When we chant, we are actualizing the teachings with our very breath and being. Our life becomes a life of trust in which each thing (even music or the words of a Zen chant) manifests as the same essential reality.

This is considered the case whenever Zen sutras or other Buddhist chants such as *dharanis* and *mantras* are recited because the ultimate purpose of chanting is not just to chant but to purify the mind and experience realization. In other words, the purpose of chanting is to reach *samadhi* or unity of mind and body in activity. Through recitation we realize that we are buddhas at the very same time we are chanting their names as objects of

---

29. Asociación Zen Taisen Deshimaru, "Kesa: The Monk's Robe," para. 3.

devotion. It is apparent, then, that as Chris Pauling points out in *Introducing Buddhism*:

> Devotional practice in Buddhism might mean something as simple and unstructured as gazing at a statue of the Buddha, and perhaps experiencing a sense of quiet peace. It might mean chanting a few traditional verses. It might mean conjuring up a colourful mental visualization. Or it might mean taking part in a dramatic and moving ritual with other people, perhaps incorporating poetry, music, readings, incense, and offerings. But whatever the form such practices take, their main purpose is always the same—to nurture and strengthen our devotion . . . in the sense of commitment to making real progress along the path, as well as devotion in the sense of a self-transcending attitude that sees the real importance of life as lying in something above and beyond our own small wants and fears.[30]

In conclusion, it is important to recognize that all of this doesn't mean that by being open to different practices we dilute our own. It doesn't mean that faith must be taken on wholesale, but that we enrich our practice by discovering the many nuances of what it means to be a Zen practitioner. In adapting Zen to the West, we can better practice and teach the Dharma by greater knowledge of the facts, especially about lesser-known elements of the Way. If we truly wish to create the best Zen to suit our needs, surely we must avail ourselves of whatever serves us well, even if that includes aspects we may not be so comfortable with.

30. Pauling, *Introducing Buddhism*, 53–54.

6

Zen Faith In Becoming A Buddha

IF WE ARE GOING to employ faith in our ability to become a buddha then it is important that we first put it in the right perspective. To get the most out of this kind of faith, it's advisable to develop an understanding of what it is and the way in which it functions. This involves taking it out of the many boxes into which it has been placed.

Take the term blind faith, for example. Faith that is blind quite rightly evokes discomfort but if we sit with the term for a while, it becomes apparent that faith in Zen has always been in some way blind, and that this is not necessarily a bad thing. It comes down to how we understand the nature and function of faith.

It is true that blind faith as in unquestioning obedience to a set of beliefs has never been a part of Zen Buddhism. Thich Nhat Hanh states that theologians might talk of a leap of faith, but the faith of Zen is not blind and not a leap.

The faith of Zen adherents, he explains, rests on our own insight and experience. We trust in our capacity to walk in the direction of the Dharma and the discoveries we make serve as the impetus to keep striving. Hanh is pointing out that in Zen we don't get anywhere in a holistic sense unless we experience something personally. Otherwise, it's just an intellectual belief.

Yet it is important to note that in one sense it is completely accurate to describe a Zen practitioner's actions as a leap of faith because anyone who begins the Path *is* that child jumping into the Dharma. All who tread the Way do so on the proviso that the Buddha was telling the truth. For a certain amount of time, we don't know for ourselves if the Way will come to fruition. In a sense, then, Buddhist faith has always been blind because it precedes seeing and knowing. It takes the Dharma or buddha nature or whatever is our object of attention and throws it out there in search of an answer.

D. T. Suzuki observed that strong faith engenders a spirit of inquiry and generates the capacity within the practitioner required for "throwing oneself down the precipice" and into the abyss created by a gap in knowledge. A leap of faith might be a tentative acceptance of the unproven but in a certain Zen sense it can also be *upaya* or skillful means; of questioning and acting when we haven't yet made our own discoveries.

Considering the above, it is prudent not to summarily dismiss Zen's leap of faith because there is no other way to step onto a Path. Since no one can master direct experience for anyone else, we must act on the promise of realization for a while until faith becomes knowledge. Faith in the Buddha's awakening (which is also faith in our own buddha nature) has to be the prerequisite for realization—there's no way around it. Thus, the leap of faith in Zen describes a particular position that we are taking rather than what we believe.

This position is a state of anticipatory confidence. It is the stance of openness we create when we want to take in experiential knowledge. It is an attitude of hope. As Amber D. Carpenter points out:

> When faith is not belief in a proposition . . . then faith is a distinctive attitude towards that object, rather than a belief maintained via a non-standard epistemological mode. The attitude itself is the central thing . . . This disposition of trusting openness precisely without tying it to some determinate outcome, is what it is to have faith in a thing or person . . . [This] cannot be blind faith, faith against all evidence, or even faith that does not ask for evidence—experience should confirm us. If it does not . . . we withdraw our trust. On the other hand, experience can only confirm if our [practice] is undertaken in the right spirit in the first place.[1]

This is where the true import of a Zen leap of faith becomes clear. We do not leap into blind assent at all but whatever we can hold in our very own hands. We are not even asked to concentrate on propositional truth claims but only what we can know in the here and now. That takes many

---

1. See Carpenter, "Faith Without God in Nagarjuna," 12.

forms. It includes but is greater than intellectual agreement. It all depends on our openness and receptiveness to the present, that is, on our faith.

Since the Buddha never employed faith as a means of accepting larger than life unprovable claims, the faith of Zen is a faith that acts as the basis of personal experience. While answers might not be immediately forthcoming, numerous sutras suggest that if we pursue the Buddha Way and maintain faith, then they can eventually come within the range of direct experience.

So, while first-hand knowledge takes time to manifest, we are asked to take a leap on the condition that it will nevertheless do so. If it does not, Zen will not hold us down and insist on belief. Zen faith derives its authority from confirmational experience, and this is a principle that affects it from its foundations upwards. From the perspective of faith in becoming a buddha we can see that in the Zen context, faith can help us draw decisiveness out of the undecided because it is a process not a set of truth claims. One of its functions or duties is to occupy that gap in time when we simply do not know. It is to continually inquire. Seen in this way, the term faith can take on a more utilitarian flavor and less of a pejorative one.

The late Zen teacher, the Reverend Master Jiyu-Kennett of the Order of Buddhist Contemplatives, saw this as the difference between *absolute faith* and *perfect faith*. Absolute faith requires us to give up our will whereas perfect faith does not. Instead, it uses volition as fuel for the journey. Absolute faith is rigid, unbending, static, and is characterized by the my way or hit the highway kind of attitude. In contrast, perfect faith is flexible and open. It doesn't take umbrage to being challenged because it cannot be pinned down to an equation or a substance.

Thus, there is a deeper aspect to this faith that we need to be aware of—there is no-thing to cling to or defend. In reality, there is always mutuality due to the interpenetration of phenomena. Absolute faith supports and defends some-thing. Perfect faith, however, as Reverend Master Kennett pointed out, is a giving and receiving, sharing, and being shared, an acceptance and being accepted. So, unlike absolute faith, perfect faith is not carried like a heavy object. It is full of lightness, acceptance, and flexibility.

Perfect faith is all of this because the intrinsic nature of reality does not rely on opposites—belief against belief. Nor does it disintegrate the moment it meets intellectual resistance. Perfect faith, as its name suggests, is perfect because it is emptiness itself. It doesn't need to insist on itself since it is always here.

The late Reverend Master Daizui MacPhillamy (also of the Order of Buddhist Contemplatives) put his own spin on these two terms. In his experience, belief was an opinion held without proof while faith is trust or confidence in something. Through practice, the latter confirms the former and because of this, it doesn't matter whether a person starts out with or without belief because Zen training ends up in the same place for both. In this way, he draws a comparison to other religions in that trustful faith becomes a real part of people's lives. Contrastingly, belief may or may not play a central role in the life of a Zen person.

Similarly, the late Kyogen Carlson, contemporary Soto Zen priest and former Abbot of Dharma Rain Zen Center, saw Zen faith as a simple thing—gentle, flexible, and not dependent upon belief systems. This kind of faith, he taught, opens the door to the experience of complete unity with the entire universe. He pointed out that, like fish within the great ocean, we are at all times sustained and supported by this unity. Realizing this unity is the mystical experience of Zen.

Real faith embraces honest doubt and requires very little in the way of belief purely because of the way in which they function in the world. Doubt in Zen, Carlson taught, is the wish to understand but not limit other people or ways of expressing the truth. When belief becomes rigid and without flexibility, he warned, real faith cannot exist. This is because the function of spiritual doubt and inquiry is to "recognize the imperfections in things, weigh them against their merits, and understand the value of a teaching or practice." The pliability of seeking implied in an honest doubt is indispensable and without it, we're "impaled on the necessity of belief."[2]

It is thus the combination of both faith and honest doubt which leads to realization. Faith allows us to see enlightenment manifesting around us and honest doubt permits us to accept human nature as it is. While the balance between them can be difficult to manage, Carlson taught that it was the only formula for a truly spiritual life.

In Theravada Buddhism, enacting this faith is called going for refuge in the Triple Gem—the Buddha, Dharma, and Sangha. The Anguttara Nikaya (The Numerical Discourses) outlines the benefits of this act of faith:

> If someone's unwavering faith is established in the Buddha, and
> if virtues favored by the noble ones are theirs, establishing faith
> in the Sangha if they have rectified their view, they are neither
> poor nor is their life useless. Therefore, the wise gain right view,

2. Carlson, *Zen in the American Grain,* 8, 11.

faith, and virtues, and establish themselves in the Dharma of the Enlightened One.

In Zen, this is formally accomplished through the vow of three refuges (also known as the three devotions or three treasures) which serve as one part of the Bodhisattva Precepts.

This act of faith is the gateway to enter the Zen path. Koun Yamada once stated that refuge is an act of devotion that arises naturally from the revelation of faith. As Dogen observed, the buddhas and ancestors of Zen all stated that receiving the precepts is the first step to entering the Way. This act of faith in the Triple Gem represents trust in the fact that an effective refuge actually exists, otherwise, why bother looking for it. The Brahmajala Sutra (Brahma Net Sutra), the sutra that the Zen Bodhisattva Precepts are based on, states that the precepts are the original source of all buddhas and sentient beings because all beings possess the purity of self-nature out of which all things, including refuge, arise.

In other words, to seek refuge is to seek ourselves because the precepts are expressions of innate buddha nature. All of you, the sutra says, should firmly believe that you are the buddhas of the future. If you always have such faith, it asserts, then the precept code is fulfilled. This demonstrates the fact that there is a relationship between the direction of attention, will and faith in the Triple Gem.

In fact, in both Theravada and Mahayana Buddhisms faith has often been praised for its value as a means of directing the mind, focusing endeavor and the development of a strong resolve.

> Faith through understanding is to listen to a teaching, understand it, and then come to a decision that there is no other teaching than this on which one can depend. Thereupon he becomes converted, and fervently tries to follow the teaching. He no longer looks to right and left, but turns to one direction, singleminded. This state of mind is faith. A sutra says: "Bodhisattva (Buddha-to-be), at his first conversion, earnestly seeks bodhi (wisdom) and is too firm to be moved." This is faith through understanding. His faith is firm and intense, based on understanding and conviction.[3]

In other words, taking refuge in the Three Treasures determines where we place our intention and motivation since faith is an operation of the human

---

3. Masutani, *A Comparative Study of Buddhism and Christianity*, 68–79.

will in which a person in full sincerity turns their aspirations and their efforts toward the attainment of Buddhist ideals.[4]

Torei, one of the most eminent Zen masters of pre-modern Japan, taught that faith is an attitude involving the will, intellect, and emotion, which unfold knowledge in stages. He stressed that these are three key factors important in the Zen notion of taking refuge since they direct our faith in a certain manner.

Torei taught that to enable practice, a Zen student first adopts an intellectual faith in the doctrines of Zen without fully understanding or experiencing their effects. Even though we mustn't rely on doctrinal vehicles, he said, we must nevertheless first take doctrine as an object of faith and the basis for cultivation. Our intrinsic enlightenment (buddha nature) must be taken on faith or as a conjecture until a certain stage is reached and that any claim of knowledge without that realization is worthless.

In the Shumon Mujintoron (The Inexhaustible Lamp of Zen), the objects of this initial faith are outlined.

> If you want to master this path, first you need the faculty of great faith. What is this faculty of faith? It means faith in the inherence of the nature of mind and the immeasurable knowledge of all Buddhas; faith that those who cultivate it will realize it, regardless of the magnitude of their potential or degree of intelligence . . . faith that when the time comes and effort has been sufficient, the enlightened nature will suddenly appear, without making use of intellectual discrimination; faith that . . . every lifetime from here on is one thing, cultivation of the way; faith in upholding the experience of progressive transcendence . . .[5]

While we are maintaining trust in buddha nature and original enlightenment, we are also in the process of putting it into practice.

In Zen faith is not just following a role model or a set of ethical guidelines. Taking refuge in the Buddha Treasure is to develop the confidence that since the Buddha was human, we can emulate him successfully. It is not expressing a profound commitment to finding the Buddha's enlightenment but our enlightenment.

It is interesting to note that when the Buddha was sitting underneath the bodhi tree *Mara* chose to attack his faith in his own nature. In Buddhism Mara is any psychological or philosophical view that obstructs liberation.

4. See Bloom, "Faith: It's Arising," 309.

5. Torei, *The Undying Lamp of Zen*, 21–20.

The Buddha's own doubts about his enlightenment potential are typical of our own doubts, but the fact that he achieved enlightenment despite these is a testament to the power of his faith.

It is also proof of the power of trust in the fact of buddha nature. Taking refuge in the Buddha is to live in the faith that we already have within us all that we need to live the Way. This is why Zen masters such as Boshan Yuaniai recommended starting the faith journey with belief in ourselves and cites the best example of this as the historical Buddha. Armed only with faith, he reminded his fellow Zen monks, the Buddha determined to find enlightenment under the bodhi tree.

To Boshan, this shows that faith in oneself, the teacher and the Way is the bedrock of Zen.

> If you can have faith, then you are a vessel [of the Dharma]; if you cannot have faith, then you are not a vessel [of the Dharma]. Practitioners who wish to enter the principle of this Great Vehicle [of the Mahayana] accomplish it through faith. This word *faith* can be shallow or profound, specious or true. You must be clear about the differences! When those who have shallow faith enter the Dharma gate, you cannot really say they lack faith, but their faith is in the Dharma gate and not in their own minds. . .When you consider your mind as the Buddha, this is genuine faith . . . You must personally verify this and put it into practice . . .[6]

The late Hsing Yun, a modern Zen master, observed that after we take refuge in the Triple Gem, our faith deepens, and our character becomes more dignified. All who take refuge in the Triple Gem, he stated, even if they do not cultivate realization in this lifetime, will eventually be liberated because they have faith and good karmic conditions.

In terms of taking refuge in the second object of faith, the Dharma, we heed the Buddha's teachings and implement it in our own lives. The refuge of Dharma asks us to be one in the dharma with all sentient beings, to penetrate all sutras, and to let wisdom be like the ocean. This treasure is ineffable so to penetrate all sutras is to be one with the dharma and to discover boundless wisdom and faith.

In Zen, faith and reverence for the sutras have traditionally been considered equal to faith and reverence towards all buddhas. The Astadasasahasrika Prajnaparamita Sutra (The 18,000-Line Prajnaparamita Sutra) states that if anyone listening and reading the sutra feels respect, affection,

---

6. Sheng-Yen, *Attaining the Way*, 10.

and serene faith for it, then they also feel that for the buddhas of the past, future, and present. This is reflective of faith placed in a way of life which springs forth from entrustment in reality.

Moreover, as expressions of our true nature, particular sutras in and of themselves, are also considered synonymous with faith in the Dharma. The Mahaparinirvana Sutra (Sutra of the Great Decease), for example, states that just as all rivers flow to the sea, all sutras and all forms of meditation lead ultimately to the Mahaparinirvana Sutra since it expounds in the "most excellent manner" the doctrine of faith that all sentient beings possess buddha nature. When faith arises, it tells us, it is synonymous with respect for this sutra. Moreover, when we accord with the sutra, we can clearly see it by virtue of the power of faith, and when we ground ourselves in that faith, we gain the nature of an enlightened person.

The Surangama Samadhi Sutra (Samadhi of the Heroic Progression) states that if a person hears this sutra and has faith in it, reciting it and understanding its doctrines, preaching it for people and practicing it according to how they have preached it, then such a person will reside in the dharma of the buddhas. Profoundly residing in their faith, that person will also be protected by the buddhas.

Furthermore, such is the power of faith in this sutra that when a person resides in samadhi they perform the practice of faith for sentient beings and neither regress nor fail in the turning of the wheel of the dharma. The sutra asserts that if anyone can accept it in faith without becoming discouraged, upset, or frightened by it, the blessings accruing from this will surpass those of anything else.

As for taking refuge in the third object of faith, the Sangha, it is not just to respect and uphold the guidance of the Buddhist community but to realize the kinship of all things. In Zen everything is considered a teacher because the universal Sangha is the community of sentient and insentient beings. *Sankie* or the threefold refuge chant in Zen is taken from the Saddharmapundarika Sutra (Lotus Sutra) and expresses three aspects of faith in The Sutra, that is, universal emptiness.

> We return home to the Buddha. Together with all sentient beings may we realize the Great Way and evoke the Mind most high. We return home to the Dharma. Together with all sentient beings may we delve deep into the sutras and be wisdom vast as the great ocean. We return home to the Sangha. Together with all sentient beings may we be the Great Assembly and may all things be completely free.

This illustrates the fact that some Buddhists consider Zen faith and the Triple Gem as having two facets. Outer refuge refers to the way in which they role model how a person of faith reaches enlightenment or how a fully enlightened person behaves. Inner refuge is to take faith in the Triple Gem as expressions of differing aspects of reality within all things and as all things. "Going out and returning" or "constantly returning" in Zen specifically refers to this act of returning again and again to the Triple Gem as an expression of buddha nature.

This perfect faith is exemplified by the relationship between student and master. Dogen emphatically stated that if right faith arises in our mind, we should practice with a master. To have a mind of faith is to be deeply engaged with the teachings, the practice, and life as a whole. To trust in the veracity of the teachings and their embodiment in the teachers is essential.[7] As Francis Dojun Cook asserts:

> The various chapters of Shobogenzo show that there can be several objects of faith, but in the final analysis, all are the same. One has faith in the Buddha, and one must have faith in one's teacher— one's teacher is a kind of surrogate Buddha inasmuch as he has inherited the Buddha's mind from his own teacher, and so on, back to the time of Shakyamuni himself. This is the meaning of the ancestral succession in the lineage of teachers. One must also have faith in the teachings of Buddhism—but are these not merely verbal expressions of the Buddha mind? And one must have faith in one's own intrinsic Buddha nature. This faith is the very door through which one enters the Dharma.[8]

It is for this reason that Dogen believed that the person without faith is like a broken jug. For Dogen faithless people cannot be vessels of the teaching.

Wonhyo in his Gisillon So (A Commentary on the Awakening of Mahayana Faith) outlined four types of faith which stress the importance of a student's attitude toward Buddhist education as a key factor for success. The first is that we must have faith that the truth of suchness is the fundamental basis of our actions. Second, we must have faith in the virtue of Buddha, and try to seek buddha-wisdom. Third, we must have faith in the profits and results of Dharma and try to practice its moral directives. Fourth, we must have faith in the Sangha and try to learn from its teaching and practice.

7. Kinst, *Trust, Realization and the Self in Soto Zen Practice*, 64.
8. Cook, *How to Raise an Ox*, 21.

These also describe the recommended mind state of students in the following three ways. First, students should show faith and respect to the teacher. Second, students should have faith that they can attain their goal through the guidance of their teacher. Lastly, students should have faith they can contribute to the welfare of other human beings by attaining their educational goal.[9]

Taking refuge in our own nature is also to have faith in the buddha nature of the teacher. Whatever they have realized, so can we. It is not a matter of ego that we can actually go "eyebrow to eyebrow" with the ancestors but a matter of faith. Dogen himself became enlightenment itself when he heard his teacher say, "Body and mind must fall away." This was an act of profound faith and exemplifies the fact that faith is more than the foundation for practice and gateway to the Dharma, it is the practice itself. It is a complete willingness to let go.

Thus, if we conceive of religions as paths to a goal, we then naturally find ourselves thinking in terms of sequences of actions (practices deemed efficacious) for moving from an original state to a desired state.[10] This concept of stages of sustained faith is common to all schools of Buddhism, and indeed, most religions. Hence, we find Buddhist texts suggesting that we build faith up over time.

The well-known Zen oxherding pictures illustrate this process. These are a series of short poems and accompanying pictures used in Zen to illustrate the stages of progression toward realization, the recognition of unity, and the subsequent return into the world with a newfound integration of differentiation in oneness. The oxherd symbolizes the separate self and the ox essential nature. In these pictures they are at first separate, but eventually the oxherd comes to realize his fundamental identity with essential nature.

Many variations of these pictures exist. Fumyo and Kakuan's ten oxherding pictures, the ten white ox pictures by an unknown author, and the six oxherding pictures by Jitoku are among the most famous. As traditional versions of training manuals, they illustrate through pictures the spirit of Zen training and the spiritual attainment to be expected by such training.

Zenkei Shibayama, author of the seminal *A Flower Does Not Talk: Zen Essays*, explains that however many the pictures, they all point to the ultimate aim of religious life and show us the true picture of faith. The first four pictures explain a gradual disciplinary process and are generally taken to

9. Kim, "Wonhyo's Human Character Education," 154.
10. Taves, "No Field Is an Island," 181.

represent Zen training step by step. They all, however, represent one phase of that which is presented in the fifth and the six Pictures. That is, they are the gradual in the direct (or sudden) experience of awakening.[11]

Important to our discussion of stages of training is the reward of the progression through the first four stages—the fifth of Jitoku's condensed six pictures entitled *The Tether of Faith*. Shibayama defines faith as "the aspiration for the joy of awakening in the Eternal and the Absolute, the happiness of losing the self in the Buddha. It is the single-minded longing for the mind-ox."[12] A thought of faith awakens in our mind, and the author likens this to the state in which a tether has been fastened to the mind-ox which has so far been lost, having gone astray.

This fifth picture is based upon the recognition that, since the Buddha and ordinary people are connected, the mind-ox and the herdsman are related, and here arises faith. This eagerness to seek after the truth and the zeal to inquire into reality is encouraged by faith. Only after completing the prior four stages, can the tether be fastened around the ox (a thought of faith is awakened), and for the first time connect the herdsman and the mind-ox through the tether. This is the second-to-last step toward the man and the ox becoming one, since the outer self to be awakened in the inner mind-ox and thus to realize its true self.[13] The last stage of faith is known as non-retrogressive faith, also called indestructible or infallible faith.

In the Shumon Mujintoron (The Inexhaustible Lamp of Zen) Torei outlined ten stages of deepening practice which begin and end with faith, and which he took from the ten faiths (also called the ten minds or ten aspirations) of the Dasabhumika Sutra (Ten Stages Sutra). In this sutra, the Buddha describes ten stages of development that a person must progress through to accomplish full enlightenment and Buddhahood, as well as the subject of buddha nature and the awakening of the aspiration for enlightenment. It is said that all false views are subdued by the ten faiths.

While there are differing descriptions of the content and order of the ten stages of faith, in the main they are said to consist of the following: (1) a mind of faith or aspiration, (2) a mind of recollection or mindfulness (3) a mind of seminal progress or diligence (4) a mind of wisdom, or perceiving the non-substantiality of all things(5) a mind of absorption through zazen (6) a mind of non-backsliding or non-retrogressive faith (7) a mind

---

11. Shibayama, *A Flower Does Not Talk: Zen Essays,* 152–54, 157, 163–64.

12. Shibayama, *A Flower Does Not Talk: Zen Essays,* 163.

13. Shibayama, *A Flower Does Not Talk: Zen Essays,* 163–64.

of transference of merit to others (8) a mind for maintaining the dharma within oneself (9) the nirvana mind in effortlessness and (10) a mind of living in vow, performing actions in doubtless faith.

After the ten faiths, there come numerous other stages since, in the path of becoming a buddha, faith is considered a necessary step to enlightenment, but it is not until experiential wisdom is also developed that awakening occurs.

Wonhyo also differentiated between the different faith stages of "those of bodhisattva nature." He outlined two kinds of faith that practitioners embody—devotional faith and deep faith. According to Wonhyo, practitioners at a lower stage of religious development must contemplate the ten faiths. They are urged to have sincere devotion and to give themselves wholeheartedly in faith to the Tathagata to generate bodhicitta. The latter, however, have attained awareness above that of the ten faiths. They do not need to utilize them because they now have deep faith.

This deeper faith is fully embodied by those of "settled nature." Deep faith entails the awareness of emptiness and as such, involves an advanced level of wisdom and supersedes any knowledge gained in the ten faiths. Superior to devotional faith, it is thus situated higher on the path than the stages of the ten faiths. Incidentally, it is interesting to note that Wonhyo, in outlining the fact that the presence of deep faith renders the practice of the ten faiths unnecessary, is also suggesting that faith alone is adequate (or sufficient) in itself.

Consequently, if we perceive the Way as consisting of a series of progressive steps until we reach enlightenment, then it goes without saying that the faith of Stage 1 is of a different nature and intensity to that of Stage 10. Stage 1 represents an initial and undeveloped faith whereas Stage 10 is a well-developed faith fully grounded in practice, experience, and knowledge. When faith is complete, it is said that a person enters the stages of the Bodhisattva path itself. This is what Wonhyo would then call the stage of deep and sufficient faith.

This is also why it is sometimes said in Zen that all the precepts really boil down to one—I take refuge in the Buddha. Returning to who we truly are is to have deep faith and confidence in the fact that the Buddha is our natural home. This kind of faith is also known as right view which in turn equates with right faith. Right view is the understanding of suffering and its causes. Similarly, right faith is the same understanding conjoined with a confidence in the path to overcoming suffering.

Unsurprisingly, right view is at the beginning of the eightfold noble path, the Buddhist ethical action plan for how to live a realized life. The eight elements of the path consist of right view, right intention, right speech, right action, right livelihood, right effort, right mindfulness, and right concentration. Each of these interlink to enable clear sight unencumbered by the filter of the self, the ego, opinions, preferences, aversion, and craving. They facilitate the ability to see the world as it really is rather than how we want it to be so that when a person finally develops complete faith in the Buddha, there is nothing other than Buddha. For this reason, it is sometimes said that right view is the complete eightfold path.

The Mahaprajnaparamita Shastra (Treatise on the Perfection of Great Wisdom) outlines for Zen adherents what this means in terms of faith—the understanding and assurance of the Four Noble Truths; the veneration and reverence of the Buddha's character and teachings; a sincere decision to practice the Buddha's teaching; and the realization of human morality or ethics.

The Dasheng Qixin Lun (The Awakening of Mahayana Faith) also elucidates a variety of faiths, that is, faith in the ultimate source, in the numberless excellent qualities of the buddhas, in the great benefits of the teaching, and that the Sangha members have the ability to devote themselves to the practice of benefiting both themselves and others.

Unsurprisingly, in both Theravada and Zen Buddhism faith is that which increases purity of virtue, mind, views, practice, wisdom, and knowledge of the right way. Aspects of faith which do this—acceptance of reality and provision of the motivation to overcome obstacles to enlightenment—are outlined in the Cheng Weishi Lun (Discourse on the Perfection of Consciousness-only).

> What is faith? There is faith in reality, merit, and the ability for deep tolerance and will to attainment. Mental purity is its essence. Countering faithlessness and enjoying the wholesome is its function. Furthermore, faith has three distinct aspects. The first is faith in reality. This means that one deeply believes in and accepts true events and principles as they appear as phenomena. The second is faith in the existence of merit. This means that one has profound faith in and enjoyment of the true pure merits of the three treasures. The third is faith in ability. This means that one deeply believes that all mundane and transmundane forms of wholesomeness have a power that is able to produce hope. Through this one is able to counteract those thoughts of nonbelief, and one has

a strong will to witness and cultivate mundane and transmundane forms of wholesomeness.[14]

Once someone accepts the basic principles of reality, faith is traditionally considered to have the functional power of purification.

> The essence of faith lies in belief in the reality of the Buddha's existence, in belief in the virtue of the Buddha, and in belief in the power of the Buddha. It also lies in the deep appreciation of the practitioner, in the joy of the practitioner, in the desire for enlightenment of the practitioner, and in the purity of mind of the practitioner. Faith cures doubt. Faith inspires one to find delight in goodness.[15]

Zen focuses on all of this but also right faith or view as no view because in a realized state of being, the self is not an intermediary anymore, and we no longer make fallacious assumptions of ownership and self-identity.

For it to be of any use, however, Zen holds that this resolute faith must be accompanied by what is known as *doshin,* the aspiration or desire for enlightenment. In Japanese doshin is represented by the ideographic characters of way or road, heart, mind, or faith. It is variously translated as faith in the Way, the heart of the Way, the mind's search for truth, and the will to the truth.

These expressions describe a strong drive for enlightenment and the kind of awareness or mindset which is wholeheartedly applied to everything, especially Zen practice. In the Shobogenzo (Treasure of the True Dharma Eye) chapter which specifically addresses doshin, Dogen encouraged people to deeply take refuge in the three treasures, the oneness of reality.

Doshin must occur with great faith because it is only when a strong drive for enlightenment is partnered with strong faith, that there comes the recognition of our true nature. The Erru Sixing Lun (Treatise on the Two Entrances and Four Practices) by Bodhidharma teaches that enlightenment is the realization of this truth. To Bodhidharma, realizing the truth of reality was the same as having deep faith in what the Treatise describes as "sentient beings possessing the same true nature." The implication of this, Dogen pointed out, is that everyone who trains with right faith will be enlightened equally.

14. Muller, "Right View (samyak-drsti) and Correct Faith (sraddha)," 1.

15. Yun, *Being Good: Buddhist Ethics for Everyday Life,* 173.

Since buddha nature is something that everyone is, Dogen taught that if people practice with right faith, they will all attain the Way, irrespective of the amount of intelligence they possess. As the Buddha himself said, "If the element of the truth-seeker did not exist in people, there would be no turning away from craving, nor could there be a longing for nirvana, nor a seeking for it, nor a resolve to find it." For this reason, the Buddha praised qualities such as *dhammachanda* (righteous desire) and *appamada* (alertness, attentiveness, diligence, earnestness, heedfulness, care, zeal).

Doshin, amongst other things, imbues the path with energy, endeavor, and enthusiasm. Zen places great emphasis upon this noble diligence since it removes suffering and darkness and is the basis of freedom. If we have great diligence, free from discouragement, then there is nothing we cannot attain and accomplish. So not only does doshin provide security along the Way, it is also a quality that brings knowledge of thusness. As such, the Buddha advised that those "who do not know and do not see decay and death as it really is, should be diligent to find what that knowledge really is."

The intent of right effort is clear—we must cultivate skillful faith, persistence, and positive intent if we are to win through to realization. Since doshin is irrevocably intertwined with not only practice but the true nature of things as well, we can also consider it synonymous with the intense drive and energy engendered by *daishinkon* or the great root of faith.

Rinzai Master Gaofeng Yuanmiao in his text Chanshi Chanyao (Three Essentials of Chan) was the first to officially teach great faith as one of three essentials or pillars of Zen along with great doubt and great determination. The Mahaparinirvana Sutra (Sutra of the Great Decease) confirms that this great faith is the foundation for the Way: "All that is said in these Mahayana sutras is the truths of the Way . . . if one believes in the Way, such a Way of faith is the root of faith (daishinkon). This assists the Way of Awakening . . . The Path begins with the root of faith . . . "[16]

Chinul made a frank and direct appraisal of the usefulness of great faith as the root of the Path:

> Obviously, if you are going to make a journey of a thousand miles, the first step has to be right; if the first step is mistaken, the whole thousand miles is mistaken. To enter the land where there is no artificiality, first faith has to be right; if the initial belief is mistaken,

16. Yamamoto, *The Mahayana Mahaparinirvana Sutra in 12 volumes*, 180.

then all virtues fade away. This is why a Zen patriarch said, "The slightest miss is as the distance between sky and earth."[17]

To have faith in mind thus means to have the great faith that awakening will follow when the mind returns to the root (or source) and realizes the essential unity of the ultimate. Bankei Yotaku, Rinzai master and the abbot of Ryomonji and Nyohoji in the seventeenth century, told his followers that when it comes to the truth, all of us must have faith that this realization can happen, and live in expectation of the day when we'll completely attain the Dharma Eye.

Dahui advised his students that they must enter through the gate of faith with decided faith and determination because right faith and right determination are the foundation of Buddhahood. Modern commentator, D. T. Suzuki, also stressed its importance in his *Manual of Zen Buddhism*:

> A thoroughgoing enlightenment is attained only through the most self-sacrificing application of the mind, supported by an inflexible faith in the finality of Zen . . . The necessary requirements are faith and personal effort, without which Zen is a mere bubble.[18]

The resulting state of well-being which arises from this is known in Japanese as *jakujo*—serenity or imperturbability.

Thus, great faith is more than ordinary trust. It is an unreserved, fully embodied, and sustained trust. The Japanese word for refuge is *kie*. *Ki* means to throw oneself into something and *e* to rely upon. Together they mean having enough faith in what we rely upon to be able to unreservedly throw ourselves into it. Dogen suggested that we should leap into the three treasures in the same way that a child leaps into its father's arms. If you throw yourself into the house of Buddha, he said, then the Dharma fills your hand.

We can do this because we know for ourselves that we are emptiness itself, which is also deep faith in the reality of the true self. Hakuin Ekaku, who devised rigorous training methods integrating zazen and koan practice, greatly emphasized the importance of truly knowing your own nature. Realization of this gives us the basis for a secure faith in the practice. This faith is not ephemeral, he pointed out, but real in our daily lives.

Naong Hyegeun, a Korean Zen master of the fourteenth century, observed that sudden awakening only lies within the one clear faith of the practitioner's thought.

17. Cleary, *Kensho: The Heart of Zen*, 3.

18. Suzuki, *An Introduction to Zen Buddhism*, 115.

This is why the Buddha also said, "Faith, as the root of one's fundamental being and the mother of virtue, brings about the development of the good dharma of the fundamental unity. Faith brings about the development of wisdom's virtue and faith infallibly brings one to the arrival in the seat of Vairocana" (the Dharma Body or Dharmakaya of the historical Buddha)[19]

Yasutani also described great faith in terms of this fundamental knowledge. He saw it as a very strong faith which is deeply and soundly rooted in the earth like a huge tree so that nothing can move it or uproot it. It is a faith with which we engage ourselves totally and wholeheartedly in our practice. It is the fundamental conviction of buddha nature. So, when we talk about great faith, he said, it is the fundamental faith or single-minded devotion to this very fact.

In his opinion, great faith is more applicable to the path of becoming a buddha than faith as Buddha. He classified Zen into various types with the former classed as *Daijo Zen* (Greater Vehicle, Mahayana Buddhism) and the latter Saijojo-Zen (Supreme Vehicle Zen). According to Yasutani, the purpose of Daijo Zen is enlightenment or seeing into our original nature through kensho, meditation and by the realization of the Way in our everyday life.

This combination of insight and practice in Daijo Zen has variously been described in the following combinations depending upon circumstances and the individual—sudden enlightenment followed by gradual cultivation, sudden cultivation followed by gradual enlightenment, sudden cultivation following sudden enlightenment, and gradual cultivation followed by gradual enlightenment. It goes without saying that faith is present throughout.

The primary and most well-known method of cultivating insight into our original nature in Daijo Zen is the koan. Koans are short pieces of text usually in the form of a story, dialogue, question, or statement that concerns a certain theme or understanding to be made clear. They cannot be completely understood via the intellect but by entering into the koan, not as an object outside of us, but as the seeking mind itself.

Bodhidharma taught four principles of Zen which relate to this seeking mind—that everything arises from the mind, the nature of the mind is buddha nature, all sentient beings have buddha nature, and that to realize original nature, we must observe the mind. The last principle is achieved

19. Naong, "A Letter to Minister Mok In-gil," para. 1.

when kensho occurs and our heart-mind is in union with ultimate primordial awareness itself, our indwelling buddha nature.

When subject and object are no longer two i.e., there is a state of non-duality of subject and object, the practitioner realizes the koan. All koans are manifestations of the one mind, and it is this mind that we "enter into" when duality gives way, and we break through all self-made barriers. In his Chuanxinfayao (Treatise on the Essentials of the Transmission of Mind), Huangbo Xiyun said that once he knew what the *mani jewel* (emptiness) was, he could clearly see that "all those who accept it in faith are in correspondence with it."

The Zhendaoge (Song of Enlightenment) says that anyone who faithfully receives this wish-fulfilling jewel and respectfully practices in accordance with it will certainly gain a response. That is, they will all attain the "Dharma body of all the buddhas of the ten directions," not to mention nirvana and its associated facets of permanence, bliss, true-self, and purity.

This faith relies on a gradual process of cause and effect. The causes are faith and practice, and the effect is wisdom. A verse by Yuquan Shenxiu in the Avatamsaka Sutra (Flower Garland Sutra) reminds us that the body is the Bodhi tree and the mind like a bright mirror, so always we must strive to polish it so that the dust does not settle.

This is the journey of becoming a buddha through five main methods—faith in the Way, in our ability to realize essential nature, in practice, in the buddhas and ancestors, and in the phenomenal world as a responsive agent of buddha-dharma. A different kind of faith, patriarchal faith or faith as an expression or function of buddha nature, will be the next focus of our discussion.

7

Zen Faith As Buddha

IF WE ARE GOING to understand faith as Buddha, then it is important that we first put it in the right perspective. To get the most out of this kind of faith, we need to develop an understanding of what it is and the way in which it functions. This involves clearly knowing how it is both different and complementary to faith in becoming a buddha. It is especially crucial to understand how Zen practice can be both gradual and sudden or phenomenal and essential at the same time, so that faith in original enlightenment is, in turn, the actualization of faith as Buddha.

One approach or method to realize the meaning of faith as Buddha is to experience and embody certain states and understandings. Take, for example, what is known as the mind of faith. In Zen, certain key concepts such as this reflect an understanding of faith as Buddha. The term *xin* denotes absolute trust or believing mind and will. The Chinese ideogram for xin is a combination of the characters person who speaks. It is suggestive of a person who speaks with honesty and therefore can be trusted with confidence.

Xinxin or trusting the mind captures this well. Xinxin refers to the conviction that the searching mind is the object of its own search i.e., buddha nature. In terms of a process or a practice, this faith is the experience of the mind when we experience non-duality. In this state, the trusting mind itself becomes the object of trust.

This truthful mind or the suchness of reality is already perfect and so cannot be attained or created. Dogen explained this about essential nature and faith:

> The virtue of faith in the exposition of the "Five Virtues" of faith, vigor, mindfulness, concentration, and wisdom is engendered neither by the self nor by others. Because it is generated neither by forcing oneself nor by one's contrivance, neither by being coerced by others nor by fitting in a self-made norm, faith has been imparted intimately through the ancestors in India and China. Faith is so called when the entire body becomes faith itself.[1]

For Dogen, faith that permeates the whole body is what is called true faith, which always accompanies Buddhahood. If it weren't for Buddhahood, faith would not appear.

In his Bendowa (Discourse on the Practice of the Way), he stated that acquiring the essence of the teachings and transmission necessarily depends on sincerity and faith which do not come from outside or inside. Rather, they arise through understanding the value of the teachings and transforming oneself accordingly.

This is not just a positive, generalized sense of confidence that Zen might be liberating. Rather, faith exists in the form of the purified mind— the unity of faith and wisdom. In recognition of this fact Dogen observed that:

> . . .[t]he power of faith leaves no room for self-deception or evasion. It is like how one looks back when being called by another. From the moment of birth until old age, it is always what it is. Even in great suffering, it goes away and comes back freely. Therefore, faith is like a crystal ball [that can clean and purify dirty water].[2]

Thus, this original mind is not only the perfect goal of the perfect act of faith, but also perfect faith itself since, as the Xinxin Ming (Verses on the Faith in Mind) tells us, both faith and mind are not separated.

So, while the mind of faith is generally considered to constitute the inception of the Buddhist path, at the same time, the moment we have total faith in this mind, we are that pure mind itself, the manifested Buddha, Dharma, and Sangha. It is, therefore, substantially the same as the

---

1. Kim, *Eihei Dogen: Mystical Realist*, 65.
2. Kimura, "Faith and Enlightenment in Dogen's Shobogenzo," 156.

buddha-mind (*busshin*) and is called aspiration (*hosshin*) when it begins to aspire to *bodhi*, the highest wisdom.

Accordingly, the Xinxin Ming (by the third Zen ancestor, Jianzhi Sengcan) suggests that rather than having faith in outward buddhas, we can more accurately practice by having faith in the one mind as the Buddha himself did. The term xinxin can thus refer to one of two things—faith *as* manifested mind or faith *in* the purity of our own mind, the three jewels and the principle of causality. This corresponds to what in Zen is known as realizing and having faith in the one mind. True faith in mind is the belief grounded in the realization that we have a fundamental, unmoving, and unchanging mind. This mind is the tathagatagarbha (womb of the Buddha) in every sentient being.

This is also why Zen requires us to observe the precepts without any notion of gaining something because refuge in the Buddha as the personification of wisdom is refuge in ourselves as well. We cannot have one without the other because the three treasures are both the path to the awakened mind and awakening itself since realization is not conditioned. It is innate. In the Zazen Wasan (Song of Zazen) Hakuin states that since all beings by nature are Buddha whenever we are coming and going we are never astray. Our true nature is always here.

So, we can see that because the one mind is ever present, whenever we have faith in becoming a buddha and raise total awareness of this mind, we are also embodying faith as Buddha. The Mahaparinirvana Shastra (Treatise on the Sutra of the Great Decease) says that this right faith is the "delight of True Dharma." The Shastra defines it as the unflinching faith and unperturbed abiding in the underlying reality of all things which is beyond creation and destruction. A bodhisattva is perfect in faith, it states, because perfect faith believes deeply that the Buddha, Dharma, and Sangha are perpetual.

Another Zen term, *bodaishin* (raising the bodhi mind), can also be used to further illustrate this viewpoint. This arising of the awakening of the mind, or the bodhi enlightened mind (*anuttara samyak sambodhi*) is an attribute of every buddha. It represents the development and application of a strong and purposeful determination to seek enlightenment. D. T. Suzuki described it as the turning towards enlightenment of the mind which was formerly engaged in something worldly. This fierce act of will is a necessary element for anyone who seeks enlightenment which equates with the awakened mind or the condition of the mind perceiving emptiness.

This correct faith or Mahayana faith has been described as the joyous recollection of suchness. As the Mahaparinirvana Sutra (Sutra of the Great Decease) reminds us:

> Faith is not something that is added to the worldly mind—it is the manifestation of the mind's Buddha-nature. One who understands Buddha is a Buddha himself; one who has faith in Buddha is a Buddha himself. But it is difficult to uncover and recover one's Buddha nature; it is difficult to maintain a pure mind in the constant rise and fall of greed, anger and worldly passion; yet faith enables one to do it.[3]

An act of faith is the practice of enlightenment which in turn is also an act of faith. As Chinul pointed out:

> Once you have developed right faith, it is necessary to understand it. Yung-ming said, "Faith without understanding increases ignorance; understanding without faith increases subjective opinions." So we know that we can gain access to the path rapidly when faith and understanding are combined.[4]

In this sense, there is a certain circularity to faith as Buddha. The Abhidharma Vibhasa Shastra (Great Elucidation of the Abhidharma) points out the mutually reinforcing and cyclical nature of this faith:

> What do you mean by liberation through faith? By means of faith, one can observe faith; by following faith, one can attain faith. Those sticking to the former can observe the faith in his cultivation on the basis of his faith in achieving the Way. Those sticking to the latter can achieve his faith-fruits since he continues his faith in the Way. Hence, the liberation through faith.[5]

Dogen also likened practice to a spiral. Every time we raise the bodhi mind, he pointed out, we practice, we attain realization, and we strengthen our practice. This perfect circle is mutually reinforcing and interpenetrative. To strengthen our faith, then, is to strengthen our entire practice because faith, practice, and realization are inseparable.

Shikantaza is the perfect method to illustrate this principle. *Shikan* means nothing but or just, *ta* means to strike and *za* to sit. Therefore, shikantaza is a mode of practice in which our mind is solely dedicated to

3. Bukkyo Dendo Kyokai, *The Teaching of Buddha*, 181.

4. Cleary, *Kensho: The Heart of Zen*, 4.

5. Kang, "On the Meaning of "Faith" in Early Ch'an," 98.

and absorbed in just sitting. Dogen said that when we just sit it reveals complete faith in the Way and is the heart of the teaching.

Just sitting, however, is not a kind of zazen limited to seated meditation. Sitting refers to any other action that we take in the world, even being silent. Just means that there is nothing in the world that is not sitting. This is a way of being totally aware in the world in which every facet of life, not just zazen alone, is a part of Zen training. Yasutani defined it as a highly elevated state of concentrated awareness, in which we are neither overstretched nor restless or slackened. This means that all things in the entire universe are Buddhist practice exactly as they are.

This is fully embodied faith that the self and all things in the universe are one. Since we are sitting as an enactment of buddha nature, when we sit with this complete awareness it is not us sitting but Buddha. As Dogen once said, where faith appears, the buddhas and ancestors also appear.

This is because the Buddha, Dharma, and Sangha are not objects outside oneself. The Vimalakirti Nirdesa Sutra (The Sutra Spoken by the Layman Vimalakirti) notes that:

> . . . we speak of Buddhahood, the Dharma and the Sangha as though they are three different things, but they are really only one. Buddha is manifested in His Dharma and is realized by the Sangha. Therefore, to believe in the Dharma and to cherish the Sangha is to have faith in the Buddha, and to have faith in the Buddha means to believe in the Dharma and to cherish the Sangha. Therefore, people are emancipated and enlightened simply by having faith . . .[6]

Zen faith is the faith of mutual synchronicity. Since the Buddha, Dharma, and Sangha are none other than our true nature, we must trust in them to trust in ourselves, and vice versa. When we take refuge in Buddha, he takes refuge in us.

Our zazen, then, is not only the same zazen as the buddhas but the buddhas themselves. When we go from faith in becoming the Triple Gem to fully embodying our faith by being the Triple Gem (faith as Buddha), then our trust becomes who we are. It becomes everything. As Fazang put it, when faith is complete, one becomes Buddha.

Consequently, in his Fukanzazengi (Universally Recommended Instructions for Zazen) Dogen advised meditators to have no designs on becoming a buddha. According to Dogen, true zazen is not learning

6. Bukkyo Dendo Kyokai, *The Teaching of Buddha*, 178.

meditation practice per se, but the practice-realization of totally culminated awakening. Since zazen is the essential function of all the buddhas, it is not a step-by-step program but the practice of a buddha who does not seek to make a buddha. Realization is just sitting as a kind of ritualized mode of silent inquiry.

Thus, zazen is not waiting for enlightenment, but simply the practice of buddhas. It is not concerned with special states of consciousness or acquiring something in some future time. It is simultaneously the essence, practice, and expression of enlightenment right now. This is why Tiantong Rujing, Dogen's teacher, taught that zazen is immeasurable and that shikantaza is nothing other than satori.

Jundo Cohen, author, Zen teacher and founder of the Treeleaf Zendo, a Soto Zen community using visual media to link Zen practitioners around the world, considers this faith aspect of shikantaza central to its proper understanding. In a forum article *What's Often Missing in Shikantaza Explanations* he argues that this key aspect of faith often seems to be missing, misunderstood, or understated and that by not placing faith and trust front and center (or leaving them out altogether), modern Zen robs zazen of its power "like a fire without fuel, a tiger without its claws."

> Shikantaza Zazen must be sat, for the time it is sat, with the student profoundly *trusting* deep in her bones that sitting itself is a complete and sacred act, the one and only action that need be done in the whole universe in that instant of sitting. This truth . . . must be silently and subtly felt deep down . . . [T]here only needs to be a subtle, yet vital sense and *faith*, felt deep down in the gut while sitting, that "THIS IS IT! THERE IS NO OTHER IT!." [my italics][7]

He points out that by leaving out the vital ingredient (trustful faith), explanations of Zen meditation miss the mark since they can leave students thinking of zazen as just some relaxation technique or place to sit quietly without purpose. Consequently, they may fail to distinguish shikantaza sufficiently from other meditation forms and never realize the fact that when we truly taste to the marrow the real meaning of nothing to achieve, i.e., faith as buddha, we have finally reached a great spiritual achievement.

Menzan Zuiho also warned against the dualistic meditation of those who aspire to rid themselves of delusion and to gain enlightenment. By making delusion and enlightenment the objects of attention, he pointed

---

7. Cohen, "What's Often Missing in Shikantaza Explanations," 1.

out, we create the karma of acceptance and rejection. From his point of view, zazen is not a practice for eliminating something to gain something else. Instead, we should just let the darkness itself become the self-illumination of the light.

According to the above understanding of faith, therefore, this means that we don't have to strive for jakujo—serenity or imperturbability. We are already perfectly tranquil. Since the Way is originally perfect and all-pervading, it is not contingent on practice and realization. This is why Nanquan Puyuan taught that ordinary mind is the Way.

Hee-Jin Kim, author of *Eihei Dogen: Mystical Realist* writes that for Dogen, faith lay in original enlightenment and enlightenment came from original faith. He gave examples to illustrate the mutually reinforcing nature of faith and enlightenment. One involved an elderly man who, in the Buddha's time, was able to actualize enlightenment because of his strong faith in unsurpassed awakening. In a classic Zen moment, he awakened when hit with a ball despite being in a darkened room and lacking visual acuity.

Another concerned a very devoted Buddhist who prepared a meal for a monk in return for a *teisho* (teaching) from him. The monk declined to do this and left. Yet just through the strength of her faith in the Dharma, the woman still attained realization. Moreover, when she found the monk and told him what happened, he too awakened. According to Dogen, all of this occurred due to the presence of faith.

In his Gakudo Yojinshu (Points to Watch in Practicing the Way) he wrote:

> It is imperative for those who practice the Way to believe in it. Those who have faith in the Way should know for certain that they are unfailingly in the Way from the very beginning—and are thus free from confusions, delusions, and disarray, as well as from additions, subtractions, and errors. Believing in this manner and penetrating the Way thusly, practice it accordingly. Such is fundamental to learning the Way.[8]

For Dogen faith was the very core of enlightenment. The implication of this is that shikantaza cannot be fully understood apart from faith. Without one another, both can't be fully meaningful.

Keizan agreed with this, stating that zazen just lets people rest easy in their fundamental endowment. It is not concerned with teaching, practice,

8. Kim, *Eihei Dogen: Mystical Realist*, 65.

or realization, yet it contains all three aspects. This is realization without realization and a state of non-attachment to levels of enlightenment.

From this, we can see that this kind of faith practice takes a different stance on right effort from that of the path of becoming a buddha. Faith as Buddha adds a caveat to right effort—that one must seek without seeking, that is, to seek without looking for any profit, and to practice effortless effort. As the Buddha explained, he did indeed cross the river of old age, sickness, and death by effort, but it wasn't by halting (exerting no effort) or straining (exerting too much effort).

So, seeking without seeking doesn't mean sitting around in a state of quietism waiting for something to happen. It is not passive. We don't disengage from good works, ignore the precepts, or refrain from cultivating certain characteristics and abilities. Rather, when embodying faith as Buddha, we don't make effort a separate thing and enlightenment another.

In other words, we don't center our practice around notions of what practice and enlightenment are because they are conceptual traps. There must be an effort in the sense of actualizing practice but at the same time, we must also not pursue sound and form (categories and definitions of enlightenment). We mustn't get bogged down by placing enlightenment, realization, kensho, faith, nirvana, and emptiness into concrete boxes because this is just piling one attachment upon another.

One important point of practice is to let go of everything, including Zen itself. To use the intellectual mind to find original mind is a recipe for disaster. What we can do, however, is become faith itself by arousing the mind of enlightenment. In this way, the separation between cause and effect, effort and result dissolves. The Anguttara Nikaya (The Numerical Discourses) describes this state:

> For one who is virtuous, in full possession of virtue, there is no need for the purposeful thought: 'May freedom from remorse arise in me . . . may joy arise in me . . . may rapture arise in me.' This is in accordance with nature . . . for one who is virtuous is free from these wishes.

Moreover, since faith as Buddha involves completely embodying doshin and daishinkon when the mind of enlightenment arises, we come to realize that our body is the emanation body (*nirmanakaya*), our energy and wisdom the resplendent body (*sambhogakaya*), and our genuine mind the truth body (*dharmakaya*). The Liuzu Tan Jing (Platform Sutra) points out that the threefold body is within our own self-natures. By truly inhabiting buddha nature as our own self-nature, we perfect the three bodies, that is, the embodiment of our physical, spiritual and energy dimensions.

This aligns well with what Sung Bae Park, Professor of Asian Philosophy and Religions, calls the two Zen approaches to realization—doctrinal and patriarchal faith. Doctrinal faith involves becoming a buddha, whereas patriarchal faith expresses the affirmation that we are already Buddha. The first is a preliminary to enlightenment, while the latter is itself enlightenment. Since there are these two types of faith, it is considered essential in Zen that we do not become content with just the former. In other words, we must not be content with relative perfection, but proceed to deep faith and full enlightenment with the realization of our oneness with the Buddha.

Patriarchal faith expresses an essence-function relationship. That is, practice is a function of enlightenment rather than a preliminary to it. Wonhyo explained this in his Gisillon So (A Commentary on the Awakening of Mahayana Faith), saying that the Mahayana mind is the essence of the doctrine, while awakening faith is its efficacious function. Park states that since this faith represents a non-dualistic essence-function construction of reality, it naturally affirms the inseparability of two seemingly separate but non-distinct things. In this case the buddha-mind and its active expression, faith.

Here Buddha is synonymous with the mind of sentient beings. Since the one mind pervades all, there is no distinction between the Buddha and sentient beings. So, to see into our nature is to know the buddha-mind. This is why Mazu Daoyi said that mind is Buddha. Huineng advised that we should have faith that the perceptual understanding of the buddhas is only our own mind. There is no other Buddha.

Dogen used the term *sokushin zebutsu,* mind itself is Buddha, which is synonymous with *sokushin jobutsu* or this very body is Buddha. This latter phrase is, in turn, related to the Tendai notion of *issho jobutsu,* Buddhahood in this very lifetime. What all these are describing is the fact that there is no difference between buddha mind and *shujo shin,* all-beings mind. This mind, states the Dasheng Qixin Lun (The Awakening of Mahayana Faith), includes the entirety of the phenomenal and the essential, that is, sentient beings's actual existence and their original nature.

Wonhyo also took this view. He taught that the Dharma is equivalent to emptiness which is equivalent to enlightenment. Since enlightenment is also synonymous with Mahayana it is, in turn, no different from the mind of sentient beings. Since the latter has the basic nature of enlightenment, it penetrates and functions universally throughout the universe. If people can understand this principle, Wonhyo observed, they are bound to arouse the broad and great root of faith.

Consequently, right faith in patriarchal faith has no object since it is the self-awakening of suchness which includes but is beyond the immanent and transcendent, subject and object, practice, and goal. Gihwa, a leading Korean Buddhist figure during the early Joseon era, explained that to have true faith, a person must be able to make this transition to the habit of non-abiding.

Non-abiding and Zen faith are two aspects of the same thing. Although this faith lacks an object and cannot abide anywhere, Gihwa pointed out that it is still called immovable to contrast it with object-based forms of faith which are unstable. So, while faith in becoming a buddha uses faith in the objects of faith (the Triple Gem, practice, and the teacher), faith as Buddha is one with the Buddha and has no object. In doctrinal faith, we are the subject of awakening and the Dharma its object, but in patriarchal faith, the Dharma is the subject of its own self-awakening and we are its expression.

Consequently, Professor Park in his book *Buddhist Faith and Sudden Enlightenment* argues that if we consider the teachings about faith in the Dasheng Qixin Lun (The Awakening of Mahayana Faith), as well as an understanding of the meaning of Mahayana in the East Asian Buddhist tradition, Zen faith does not always work according to a Western theological faith in subject-object construction. Rather, it follows an essence-function model.

This requires something difficult to do—to abandon our assumption that we always need a dualistic subject and object structure to think about experience. We tend to think that without categories of subject and object, the world doesn't make sense. Nevertheless, this is what the sutra asks of us.

Accordingly, Park argues, the term Mahayana should not be interpreted as a noun-object, but as a modifier that characterizes the type of faith. By implication, then, although the very nature of language requires an I to be the subject of the sentence containing "have faith in," the She-ta-ch'eng-lun should not be translated as "The Awakening of Faith *in* the Mahayana" but "Awakening Mahayana Faith." Park reminds us that patriarchal faith is not believing *in* the faith of the patriarchs of Zen but embodying the faith *of* the patriarchs.

For Linji Yixuan the term xin illustrated an intimate link between the transcendent mind and faith. This objectless faith overcomes the self-centered self by giving up all conceptions of faith. It represents the realization of anatta or no-self. As Dogen pointed out in his Shobogenzo (Treasure of the True Dharma Eye):

> Keep in mind that the root of faith in the Dharma is beyond self, beyond other, beyond any forcing of oneself, beyond anything contrived, beyond anything others have hauled up in their minds, beyond any objective rules or standards, and therefore it was Transmitted, unseen . . . What we call "faith" is a faith that is forged with one's whole being. . .Were it not based upon the perspective of Buddhahood, there would be no manifestation of faith. This is why it is said that we can enter the great ocean of Buddha Dharma by means of our faith.[9]

This is not faith in an object but the awakening of Dharma as ultimate faith.

Linji once said to his students that since their faith in themselves is insufficient, they turn to words and phrases and from them create their understanding. By faith in yourself he meant the immediate non-dualistic awakening to the self that is Buddha. The ordinary samsaric mind can only conceive of faith in dualistic terms, of objects outside oneself. This samsaric mind wants to get enlightened whereas the Buddha mind already is. In this sense, the mind is a faith object that is formless. Thus, according to Linji, not to have faith means not to realize satori or awaken to the true self.

Since there is the mutual permeation of phenomena, faith as Buddha is self as Buddha, everything as Buddha. Zen expresses this network of inter-relationships in the phrase one is all, all is one. This reflects an awareness of the inter-penetrative nature of the world and the realization of emptiness. To realize self as Buddha is to know faith at every point in our life.

Completely embodying faith and knowing that I am Buddha means always knowing the direct knowledge of suchness. This means faith is not some discrete thing we have but something we are. It is a state of awareness. Thus, profound faith is synonymous with the mental state of being able to abide in non-duality.

In the last chapter, we looked at some of the reasons why we need a teacher. In Zen it is through the process of *ishin denshin*—using mind to transmit mind or transmitting mind with mind—that transmission of the teaching occurs. This happens when both teacher and student share a realization of the Dharma and of unshakable faith in Buddha Mind.

9. Dogen, *Shobogenzo: The Treasure House of the Eye of the True Teaching,* 791.

It is commonly believed in Zen schools that a student and teacher awaken together. In the Saddharmapundarika Sutra (Lotus Sutra), the Buddha explained that the wisdom of buddhas is extremely deep and infinite, and difficult to enter and understand. For this reason, only a buddha together with a buddha can fathom reality.

The inter-relational nature of emptiness means that it is only together with others that we fully awaken. To learn from good companions and good teachings on the Way is not just half of the Way, the Buddha said, it is the whole of it. This is evidence of a very profound communication between the student and the teacher, and the maturation of the merit of the Triple Gem. In Japanese, this reciprocity is known as *kanno doko*.

Kanno means to respond to each other and *doko* means true relationship. It has been variously translated as mutual affinity and interaction, response to affinity, mystical communication of the Way, empathy and response, mutual resonance between stimulus and response, mutual attraction between buddhas and sentient beings, spiritual communion, and mystical communion.

In short, kanno doko is the recognition of the universality of the three refuges—that there is no difference between the precepts, the Triple Gem, our own buddha nature, and Zen. Guifeng Zongmi observed that if there is a sympathetic resonance (kanno doko) and reciprocal tallying between master and disciple then although a single flame may be transmitted to a hundred thousand lamps, there will be no difference between them.

In Case 52 of the Shoyoroku (Book of Serenity), Caoshan said to the elder De, "The Buddha's true reality body is like space: it manifests form in response to beings, like the moon in the water." Kanno doko, therefore, is the correspondence between the Buddha's power and our receptivity. This interactive communion of appeal and response between disciple and teacher, as well as between everything in the universe, cannot happen without arousing faith in mind i.e., the aspiration for awakening.

The Dasheng Qixin Lun (The Awakening of Mahayana Faith), a key text on faith, points out that on a phenomenal level, there is a difference between illusory perceptions of reality and suchness or the true nature of things. However, any gap can be erased through the permeation or perfuming of suchness, which responds to an individual when they enter the mind of faith and give rise to *doshin*, a desire to attain realization.

This is what Buddhists in Japan call *myoshi* or *myoshu*, mysterious guidance or incomprehensible assistance—the ever-present compassion that functions in emptiness. Thus, kanno doko is a mutually illuminating co-experience—the reception of our mind of faith by the Buddha and his response to it. When we have faith, the universe reaches out to us because it is us. When we have right faith, the Dasheng Qixin Lun (The Awakening of Mahayana Faith) tells us, it cannot do otherwise.

A further fact regarding teachers and students relates to this knowledge of suchness. That is, the necessity of a teacher and faith in them is because the true spirit of Zen is a "transmission outside of scriptures." In the Bendowa (Discourse on the Practice of the Way), Dogen taught that the realm of all buddhas is inconceivable and cannot be reached by discriminative awareness. Since we can't see it as an object, only those who embody right faith and great capacity can enter this realm.

Awakening cannot be through words or intellect but the non-duality of faith and mind. The place, the Xin Xin Ming (Faith in Mind) tells us, where faith and mind are not separated, the path of language is cut off, and there is no past, present and future. Since the truth cannot be expressed in words, our recourse is to embody non-conceptual faith and wisdom.

Wonhyo taught that the real power of this faith is shown in its ability to cut off the need for language as a vehicle for the expression of realization. In other words, we cannot reside in a state of no-self and no-view unless we have the power of correct faith which, in turn, relies on maintaining a state of non-abiding in views. This is not some type of mental quiescence, but an open, aware state of consciousness not constrained by conceptual understandings.

In the Dasheng Qixin Lun (The Awakening of Mahayana Faith) the meaning of the phrase "awaken right Mahayana faith" is that by eliminating the doubts caused by "misconstruing person and dharmas to have a self," we can awaken. In other words, right faith involves:

> . . . the ability to discard conditioned consciousness, thereby facilitating the true nature of reality . . . [F]aith in its ultimate sense is the ability to free oneself from any conviction, to overcome fear and drop into the abyss of the un-cognized. Thus, when regarded as a phenomenological description of the practitioner's mind, faith infers a state of non-duality, which is the hallmark of Zen practice.[10]

10. Joskovitch, "The Inexhaustible Lamp of Faith," 331.

The importance of this sutra, therefore, is not only in its promotion of Zen doctrine but more specifically in where that faith rests, that is, in the mind of sentient beings.

For this reason, in Zen non-conceptual faith is called the incomparable, unequaled, supreme faculty of awareness. The Xinxin Ming (Verses on the Faith in Mind) paints a picture for us:

> The ultimate end of things where they cannot go any further is not bound by rules and measures: In the Mind harmonious [with the Way] we have the principle of identity in which we find all strivings quieted; Doubts and irresolutions are completely done away with, and the right faith is straightened; There is nothing left behind, there is nothing retained, all is void, lucid, and self-illuminating; There is no exertion, no waste of energy—this is where thinking never attains, this is where the imagination fails to measure.

Hence, even though the Dharma is inexpressible, we can nevertheless realize it because faith as Buddha can help bridge the self-made gap between suchness and intellectual constructs.

Unsurprisingly, this affirmation of our own original Buddhahood necessarily involves the transformation of our consciousness or what is known as the revolution or transmutation of the basis (of buddha nature). Since buddha nature (the matrix of the Tathagata) is equal to ultimate truth, when we realize buddha nature, it means that this transmutation of the basis (i.e., realization) is non-backsliding or non-retrogressive. It includes but is not dependent on will and reason since it is grounded in reality and unity as a function of the one mind.

Since an irreversible transformation of the basis results in a deep, qualitative change, an enlightened person cannot fall back to the state of an unenlightened sentient being in the sense that they are irrevocably changed by realization. Once it has happened, we cannot un-know what we know. This does not negate the need for practice, but it does mean that we never again completely rely on written texts for true knowledge but on a special transmission outside the scriptures. Perhaps this is why Korean Zen master Hyujeong (also known as Seosan Daesa), author of the famous Korean text Son'ga Kwigam (The Mirror of Zen), taught that lacking faith in one's own nature is the sickness of those attached to scriptural authority.

Chinul also placed great emphasis upon the importance of this non-retrogressive faith. He pointed out that a sentient being of great aspiration who relies on the Mahayana approach has firm faith and understanding of impermanence, that his own mind is the buddha-mind, and that his own nature is the dharma-nature. Through this knowledge, a person knows how to view the vagaries of life and to draw on the purity of their own buddha nature. This gives the freedom of knowing that despite all the hardships of this world, there is no danger of backsliding.

This is a profound and unshakable faith in emptiness which, in itself, is the practice of the truth as it really is. In this way, profound faith and profound understanding are equated with enlightenment and practice, and faith the simultaneous occurrence of cultivation and enlightenment. To enter profound faith is to enter one's true nature at the same time. Zen faith is to abide firmly with resolute conviction in a state of clearness, tranquility, and freedom.

The implication of this can readily be seen if we once again look back at the stages of becoming a bodhisattva. If we perceive the Way as consisting of a series of progressive stages until we reach enlightenment, we progress through from the faith of Stage 1 that of Stage 10. If, however, we consider that faith as Buddha equates with the realization of suchness, then the mind of faith at the beginning of the fifty-two stages and the mind of wisdom at the end are the same.

The Avatamsaka Sutra (Flower Garland Sutra) describes how this occurs in the mind of faith at the beginning of the ten faiths:

> If enlightening beings can unite with such contemplations, they will not entertain a dualistic understanding of things; and all enlightening teachings will become evident to them: at the time of their first determination they will immediately attain complete perfect enlightenment, will know all things are the mind's own nature, and will perfect the body of wisdom and understand without relying on another.[11]

This means that at the initial stage a person can have a perfect realization that all things or teachings are none other than the self-nature of the mind. Thus cause (faith) and the effect (Buddhahood) are two mutually conditioning elements in a non-linear totality.

This was also one of Chinul's fundamental teachings—that at the time of the first arousal of *bodhicitta,* or thought of enlightenment, the bodhisattva realizes that they abide in the abiding-place of the buddhas and has

11. Cleary, *Entry into the Inconceivable: An Introduction to Hua-yen Buddhism,* 402–3.

their same wisdom nature. This realization constitutes his formal initiation as a bodhisattva.

Accordingly, while Shenxiu in the Avatamsaka Sutra (Flower Garland Sutra) spoke of keeping the mind like a bright mirror free from dust, the sixth Zen ancestor, Dajian Huineng, did not take this doctrinal approach. Instead, true to patriarchal faith, he taught that the mirror has no stand because buddha nature is always clean and pure. Where, then, is there room for dust?

Chinul wrote extensively on this principle saying that in patriarchal faith, the individual realizes that even in his present deluded state he is, and has always been, a perfect buddha. Buddha nature is recognized as the fundamental, eternal, and original pure nature of all things which abides as an innate principle. By understanding this fact at the very beginning of the spiritual quest (at the first of the ten levels of faith), the student becomes fully endowed with the wisdom and compassion of Buddhahood.

In his Bendowa (Discourse on the Practice of the Way), Dogen taught that since practice and enlightenment are the same, a beginner's wholehearted practice of the Way is exactly the totality of original enlightenment. He pointed out that the Way is the Way, whether at the time of the initial desire for enlightenment or the culmination of enlightenment.

He stressed that at the beginning, the middle, and the end it is equally the Way. So, although there is a progressive course of advancement through the ten levels of faith, one who brings contemplation to perfection realizes that the mind of faith throughout the ten levels also equates with a simultaneous, comprehensive understanding. As Hyujeong pointed out, the cause of Buddhahood already contains the fruits of all the stages of the path including enlightenment itself. In other words, all stages of the path are already contained with a single act of initial faith.

Likewise, Li Tongxuan, a lay scholar who was an important figure in the development and popularization of Huayan thought, claimed that the fifty-two stages were only expedient means, and in reality, each level is identical with Buddha, and Buddha is identical with all levels. As Li says:

> If they do not believe that their body and the Buddha's body are non-dual in terms of cause and effect in the stage of the ten faiths, they cannot establish [firm] faith and understanding. Therefore it is said in the chapter The Tathagata's Manifestation, "Bodhisattvas should know that a moment of their own mind contains all buddhas from the ten directions who attain right enlightenment and turn the wheel of correct dharma. Why is it so? The Buddha's mind

and their minds are non-dual." Only when you have such faith can
it be called faith.[12]

This means that at the beginning of the spiritual path a bodhisattva already
accomplishes all the merits of the subsequent stages. No one stage is privileged over another when it comes to faith.

This brings in another aspect of faith as Buddha—the relationship
between the phenomenal and essential. The Dasheng Qixin Lun (The
Awakening of Mahayana Faith) states that the one mind has two aspects—
the suchness aspect and the arising-ceasing aspect. In the phenomenal
(arising-ceasing) sense, there is certainly a difference between a beginner
and a master. Yet this represents only a partial understanding of the function of faith.

Zen faith is not just a temporary substitute eventually replaced by
wisdom. It should also be understood as an aspect of ultimate reality. So
in terms of the ultimate truth, the stages are inseparable. This is why at the
first stage the practitioner can also be considered completely enlightened.

From this, we can see that, in terms of the two truths, the gradual path
of becoming a buddha represents a phenomenal viewpoint whereas faith as
Buddha represents an essential viewpoint. From the conventional aspect,
practice is instrumental but from the essential or ultimate perspective, it is
non-instrumental.

In the Shumon Mujintoron (The Inexhaustible Lamp of Zen) Torei
defended this notion saying that the moment we give rise to the aspiration
for enlightenment we immediately attain perfect awakening. This is because seeing our true nature clarifies and enables realization. Other schools
stress the predominating conditions of merit accumulated from previous
lives, he pointed out, whereas in the Zen tradition in "an instant of single-
minded faith" we are already inside the gate of realization. Thus, Huangbo
once said, "The true Buddha is not a buddha of stages." In terms of teaching, therefore, a gradual path aims at awareness in incremental steps, but in
terms of absolute nature, the first stage includes all the other stages.

The Avatamsaka Sutra (Flower Garland Sutra) points out that the
qualities of a single thought of a bodhisattva who has aroused the first
thought of enlightenment are deep and extensive, without boundaries. In
this state, there is what is known as *inga ichinyo*, a term taken from Hakuin's
Zazen Wasan (Song of Zazen) meaning the oneness of cause and effect.

12. Koh, *Li Tongxuan's (635–730) Thought*, 40.

In the *Three Pillars of Zen* Yasutani taught the following about inga ichinyo:

> From the commencement of practice one proceeds upward in clearly differentiated stages which can be considered a ladder of cause and effect. The word inga, meaning cause and effect, implies both degree and differentiation, while ichinyo signifies equality or sameness or oneness. Thus while there are many stages corresponding to the length of practice, at every one of these different stages the mind substance is the same as that of a Buddha. Hence we say cause and effect are one.[13]

Chinul wrote that since right faith is patriarchal faith, it does not place emphasis upon cause and effect. Rather, it stresses faith in the fact that there is no need to search elsewhere. Thus, if anyone on any of the stages of the ten levels of faith believes that there is a distinction between the causal state (gradual practice) and effect (enlightenment), then they have not realized the perfection of faith supported by wisdom.

In the path of faith as Buddha, both cause (the arising of faith) and result (enlightenment) are simultaneous. Enlightenment is not produced by a producing cause (practice) but arises as innate wisdom. In the Zhengdaoge (Song of Enlightenment), a poem much favored by Zen, Yongjia Xuanjue wrote that the great void completely banishes cause and effect. Likewise, in the Zazen Wasan (Song of Zazen) Hakuin noted that "those who turn about and bear witness to self-nature, self-nature that is no-nature, go far beyond mere doctrine. Here effect and cause are the same."

When questioned about practicing to attain enlightenment by one of his students, Dogen introduced them to the term shusho itto, the oneness and equality of practice and realization. This is usually considered synonymous with *honsho myoshu*. *Honsho* means intrinsic enlightenment; *myoshu*, subtle practice. In other words, true enlightenment is itself excellent practice. There is no separate cause and effect as such.

It follows, therefore, that since practice right now is practice-realization, the practice of the mind first aroused to seek realization is the whole body of realization. All our qualities as buddha are fully manifested even when we are just starting to practice the Buddha Way. This, in turn, means that realization and practice are not confined to cause and effect.

Sally King, author and academic, points out that the stages of faith and Buddhahood are identical because, in their mutual conditioning, both

13. Kapleau, *The Three Pillars of Zen*, 57.

are seen to be empty. This means that there is no progression from cause to effect because all events are both cause and effect. If we acquire one of the stages, we acquire all of them.

Yet, if this is the case, why then, do we have stages at all? This was the burning question behind Dogen's journey of faith—if we are originally enlightened, why do we need to practice? The answer is that although the inconceivable dharma is abundant in each person, the true mark of Zen faith is that it is actualized in practice. Dainin Katagiri, a modern Soto Zen master, explains:

> Just continue to sow good seeds from moment to moment. This is zazen, which is called shikantaza, in which all delusions, doubts, distractions drop off. This kind of zazen is exactly Buddhist faith. Buddhist faith is not an idea. It is practical action we have to actualize. Even though we can explain what Buddhist faith is, what zazen is, through and through, finally there is a little bit we cannot explain. This is the core of zazen or of faith. This is the core of being. . .something we have to actualize in our daily living through our body and mind. Religious faith can become something dangerous that hurts people, so we have to polish our knowledge, polish our perceptions through and through. Then this is Buddhist faith, which is based on emptiness.[14]

Due to buddha nature, the Dharma can be proved by any human at any time provided they make the effort to do so. As the Buddha explained, the Dharma is "visible right here, immediate, inviting us to come and see, accessible, to be personally known by the wise."

So even though we might establish a moment of total insight and faith or what is known as being born in the family of the tathagata, we must continue to practice until that faith is a steady and constant way of being in the world. Enlightenment always exists during zazen but manifests only to the degree to which the practitioner matures in their practice. This means that there is a correlation between the maturity and strength of practice and the power of intrinsic enlightenment to grow in its ability to illuminate and transform experience.

At a superficial level, therefore, it might seem confusing that we have two forms of faith acting simultaneously—faith in the Way and faith as the Way. However, with a deeper understanding of what these two involve, we can see that they are not contradictory but simultaneously complimentary

14. Bercholz and Kohn, *An Introduction to Buddha and His Teachings*, 245–46.

and true. If we are going to awaken (faith in becoming a buddha), we must completely embody faith which, in turn, is the realization of buddha nature (faith as Buddha).

What this all means, therefore, is that stages on the Path are not isolated from who we really are. Nor are they separate from other Zen practices and virtues, as we will see in the next chapter. As Wonhyo observed, to have faith means to conclusively affirm the state of things and that when one attains realization through practice, it brings boundless virtue and merit.

8

Faith And Its Near Neighbors

THE IMPORTANCE OF FAITH in Zen is reflected in the fact that in whatever way it is conceived, it is not in isolation from other key aspects of Zen life. Contrary to what we in the West might imagine, faith is not a minor element of the Path shelved in some corner section of the Dharma. It is front and center amidst core teachings about key attributes and virtues. Faith is intimately connected with other facets of the Dharma.

Bodaishin (*bodhicitta*) or the great root of faith is a good example, especially when we consider raising the bodhi mind. As mentioned previously, one aspect of great faith is the development and application of a strong and purposeful determination to seek enlightenment. So important is this sustained effort of faith, that there is a multitude of terms for it, each emphasizing its own perspective. In addition to doshin and bodhaishin, for example, we have *adhyasaya*, determination or resolution, which is also used to describe the intention of the bodhisattva to liberate all beings from suffering.

Adhyasaya is one of the *satta bojjhanga* or seven factors of enlightenment which are seven qualities that both lead to enlightenment and describe enlightenment itself. In the Aksayamatinirdesa Sutra (The Teaching of Aksayamati) it is taught that the determination of the bodhisattvas is imperishable. Since adhyasaya is essentially eternal and perpetual, the sutra states that because of clear discernment and knowledge, it is the determination of perfected vows and freedom from conceit, pride, haughtiness, self-conceit, self-esteem, the pride of modesty and illusory pride.

The Pali word for this effort is *virya* which can be translated as zeal or diligence. Virya is derived from *vira*, which means hero. To have determination or resolution is to make a heroic effort with a warrior's determined zeal. Virya operates in conjunction with six other sets of enlightenment-related states. These mental capacities are so highly valued as part of Buddhist practice that they are known as inner wealth.

They are mindfulness or the recognition of both the phenomenal and essential, investigation of reality, joy or rapture, relaxation or tranquility of both body and mind, concentration or a calm, one-pointed state of concentration of mind, and equanimity, to be fully aware of all phenomena without grasping or rejecting them.

Thus, in arousing the aspiration for enlightenment, we also arouse the great faith mind that sees and recognizes impermanence because they are one and the same. Muso Soseki, a famous writer and Rinzai monk, taught that deep aspiration for enlightenment is the development of the mind that has faith in supreme enlightenment. It is faith as Buddha.

So, in addition to encapsulating various supportive elements of practice such as adhyasaya, bodaishin (raising the bodhi mind of faith) is also suchness or the one mind. This means that, on an essential level, faith is synonymous with numerous virtues and qualities. This, the Xinxin Ming (Verses on the Faith in Mind) tells us, arises from the natural and objective fact that faith and mind are non-dual.

Non-duality is faith in mind because the non-dual mind is one with the trusting mind. This is great faith as a state of consciousness; the quality of awakening inherent in the mind that the bodhisattva seeks to activate or manifest. It is this second aspect that lends itself most to a discussion of various attributes connected to faith.

For example, an awareness of non-separation i.e., to embody faith as Buddha also means that a bodhisattva recognizes the buddha nature of every person which, in turn, leads to the knowledge of the basic equality of all people. The Mahaprajnaparamita Shastra (Treatise on the Perfection of Great Wisdom) takes note of this.

> When the bodhisattva has obtained this high aspiration (adhyasaya), he equalizes his mind in regard to all beings. Beings always love their friends and hate their enemies, but, for the bodhisattva who has obtained the high aspiration, enemy and friend are equal; he regards them as the same.

This is what the Zhengdaoge (Song of Enlightenment) refers to as *byo-doshochi*, the wisdom of equal nature. It is the wisdom that all things are essentially equal and the same. Zen schools designate this knowledge of absolute equality as one of the four kinds of wisdom, four types of wisdom with which our essential nature is intrinsically endowed. The result of right faith and right view is that compassion and wisdom become the twin weights balancing the scales of enlightenment.

An early text, the Cariyapitaka Atthakata (Commentary on the Basket of Conduct), explains that compassion is a natural manifestation of faith in mind.

> An enlightened person is naturally endowed with a compassionate nature and disposition. He desires to alleviate the suffering that beings suffer . . . without ever becoming disenchanted with all the suffering in the round of existence, all for the sake of the welfare of other beings.

The implication of this for practice is clear. If we give rise to faith, we will naturally realize the wisdom and mercy of all buddhas and be able to act as a buddha.

This tells us that bodhisattvas carry out right action because they know that enlightenment occurs together with the enlightenment of others. The Vimalakirti Sutra (Sutra of the Layman Vimalakirti) teaches us that the result of this is empathy and compassion.

> The Spirit of Buddha is that of great loving kindness and compassion. The great loving kindness is the spirit to save all people by any and all means. The great compassion is the spirit that prompts it to be ill with the illness of people, to suffer with their suffering. 'Your suffering is my suffering and your happiness is my happiness,' said Buddha, and, just as a mother always loves her child, He does not forget that spirit even for a single moment, for it is the nature of Buddhahood to be compassionate.[1]

We can only end our own suffering when we are in right relationship with others. So, in arousing the aspiration for enlightenment, we also arouse the exact same mind which vows to save all beings. Faith, vows, and practice are a prescription for total well-being.

Dogen pointed out that since arousing the aspiration for enlightenment also arouses the mind that vows to save all others before attaining

---

1. Bukkyo Dendo Kyokai, *The Teaching of Buddha*, 15.

one's own liberation, it is identical to the ultimate. In other words, since pure faith transcends duality, an instant consciousness of faith, or what is known as *ichinenshin* (a single thought-moment), necessarily results in awakening. This is why the Xinxin Ming (Verses on the Faith in Mind) states that when we realize the bodhi-mind our doubts and irresolutions vanish, and life in true faith is possible.

Dogen taught that from the very first, this bodhi-mind, the raising of this vow with our whole body and mind, is itself the beginner's mind. At the same time, this raising or practice of the beginner's mind is itself *honsho*, intrinsic realization. When pure faith appears, he observed, it changes others just as it changes us, and its benefits encompass all beings.

In fact, many of the terms used in Zen practice such as *hotsumujoshin* (awakening the supreme mind), *hotsubodaishin* (awakening the bodhi-mind), *daishugyo* (great cultivation) and *jinshininga* (deep faith in causality) are also referring to this simultaneous application and embodiment of faith. The nature of vows is the same nature as faith because Zen vows are expressions of deepest reality.

Not only that, vowing is also the practice of sustaining our beneficial expressions and is a vital conative part of practice. To live a vow is to live in enduring faith. Vows are based in faith since it is only after our faith has become strong that we can generate a vow strong enough to attain awakening. Torei taught that the right way of practice is based on vow. Those with deep vow-power are not dissuaded by unauthentic or confused teachings while those with weak vow-power will encounter many obstacles.

Thus, like faith, a vow relies on doshin and adhyasaya. It is based on the exact same determination and diligence. As Zen teacher Robert Aitken pointed out, to live the mind of faith-vow is to experience numerous other things such as wonder and gratitude, and a sense of connection which engenders sympathy and affection. Faith and confidence as indispensible parts of spiritual practice cannot help but include reverence and gratitude. When there is faith and confidence, the result is a totality of being and direction.

Other practices and virtues also stem from faith. Since good faith is always reflected in physical, verbal, and mental action, it is often described as the basic principle of all virtuous deeds or, as T. W. Rhys Davids so eloquently put it, the basis of a righteous edifice. This is because as faith springs up in the kokoro, it breaks through the five hindrances—desire, malice, mental sloth, spiritual pride, and doubt. Free from these hindrances, the kokoro becomes clear, serene, untroubled.

Many sutras and masters in the Mahayana tradition outline the concordance between the development of faith and the development of virtue. Yongjia Zhenjue, in his *Sword of Wisdom* clearly stated that with sudden enlightenment to tathagata Zen, the six paramitas and myriad means are complete within that.

The Maharatnakuta Sutra (Sutra of the Heap of Jewels) equates the controlling faculty of faith with the ability to practice charity, abandon all malicious qualities, and to follow moral guidelines without obstinacy. In the Dasheng Qixin Lun (The Awakening of Mahayana Faith) five virtuous practices which enable bodaishin, the Way-seeking mind, are explored— the practices of charity, observance of precepts, patience and zeal, and the cessation of illusions. It warns us that the door will not be opened to those who are skeptical or who lack faith.

The Ratnagotravibhaga (Manual of the Ultimate Doctrine) notes that when the practice of faith in the doctrine of the Mahayana is combined with wisdom, meditation and compassion, an antidote to the hindrances of self, suffering, indifference to the welfare of others, and enmity is produced. Having practiced these four antidotes, a person attains the four kinds of supreme virtue namely, purity, unity, bliss, and eternity; they become the children of the Buddha. Faith is the guiding factor of charity, morality, and religion in the sense that it precedes all charitable, moral, and spiritual instincts and dispositions.

This is supported by the Trimsika-karika (Thirty Verses) and the Mahayana Satadharma Prakasamukha Shastra (Lucid Introduction to the One Hundred Dharmas) which position faith as the prerequisite for profitable qualities such as vigor, equanimity, and a lack of hostility. They teach that morality and right conduct nourish the tathagatagarbha, the buddha nature potentiality within everyone. Since faith in right conduct is faith in the essence of suchness, it is also the cause or medium of bodhicitta, the wish to attain enlightenment motivated by great compassion for all sentient beings.

Representing the Zen view, Dogen's Shushogi (The Significance of Cultivation and Verification) tells us that there are four kinds of wisdom which arise from the bodhi mind and which benefit others: offerings, loving words, benevolence, and identification. This last aspect is virtually synonymous with faith in mind. Dogen points out that benevolence is all-encompassing, equally benefiting oneself and others. Identification equates with non-differentiation, that is, to make no distinction between self and others.

The Vajracheddika Sutra (Diamond Sutra) also asserts that those who arouse even one thought of pure faith are all known to the tathagata and are recognized by him as having acquired an immeasurable amount of merit and virtue. Thus, when they hear the sutra spoken, they will experience the serenity of faith, even if it is for no more than a single thought.

There is a caveat to this, however. As Chinul pointed out, the bodhisattva precepts of Zen call this nature the mind ground because it grows all virtues. These virtues are inherent, he said, but they are often not manifest because they are covered by delusion. Once delusion is recognized as empty, the virtues appear. Our perceptive mind is already luminous and shining brightly but we color it with our attachments.

Since the intrinsically luminous mind has only been obscured by adventitious defilements which are not permanent in nature, ignorance is a product of a lack of faith in buddhahood rather than a lack of inherent buddhahood. Thus, virtuous qualities do not come from outside but are inherently here. As Chinul noted:

> The fourth Patriarch of Zen said to Zen Master Lazy Jung, "All the countless facets of the Teaching ultimately refer to the heart; infinite virtues are all in the mind source. All modes of discipline, concentration, and knowledge, all spiritual powers, and miraculous projections, are inherent, not apart from your mind."[2]

Chinul took care to reinforce the idea that, by the good motive of faith, all the virtue and merit of the buddhas can accord with ours without the slightest difference. He pointed out that, no matter how short a time we mobilize true faith, the virtue and merit is too great to be explained by any kind of analogy.

> Faith is the prerequisite of all good qualities—a procreator of them, like a mother who then protects and increases them. It clears away doubts, frees you from the four rivers [ignorance, attachment, craving and wrong views], and establishes you in the prosperous city of happiness and goodness. Faith cuts through gloom and clarifies the mind. It eliminates pride and is the root of respect. It is a jewel and a treasure. Like hands, it is the basis of gathering virtue. It is the best of feet for going to liberation.[3]

2. Cleary, *Kensho: The Heart of Zen*, 27.

3. Tsong-Kha-Pa, *The Great Treatise on the Stages of the Path to Enlightenment*, 80.

In other words, faith is the guide, the mother, the producer, the protector, and that which increases of all virtues. Agreeing with this, the Brahmajala Sutra (Brahma Net Sutra), the Mahayana sutra that the Zen bodhisattva precepts are based on, says that all practice stems from faith and all virtue is rooted in it.

For this reason, both Mahayana and Theravada sutras liken faith to such things as a staff, a root, a boat that will ferry one across the flood of wrong views to safety, a strong branch to lift one on to a giant tree of virtue when pursued by the wild oxen of passions, the door that shuts out the serpent of disbelief, a strong cable that holds a ship to its anchor in stormy weather, one's power, and one's wealth.[4] These are metaphors for the action and potential of faith in the development of virtue.

It is also why the paramitas (the six perfections) of Zen only become true perfections when they are enacted with the motivation of great faith. These perfections refer to the perfection or culmination of six key virtues that characterize an enlightened state. They define and give content to the thought of enlightenment. They are the perfections of charity (*dana*), moral discipline (*sila*), patience (*ksanti*), diligence (virya), meditation (*dhyana*), and wisdom (prajna).

In the section on practicing faith in the Dasheng Qixin Lun (The Awakening of Mahayana Faith), five practices for obtaining faith are explained: the practice of charity, the precepts, patience, zeal, and the practice of cessation and observation. This is nothing other than the six perfections because the practice of cessation and observation connects, in terms of its nature, to ultimate wisdom.[5]

The Mahaparinirvana Sutra (Sutra of the Great Decease) also notes the relationship between faith and the perfections. It states that Buddha-nature is called the great faithful mind because it is through a faithful mind that bodhisattvas attain the six perfections. On a phenomenal level, a perfection such as charity, for example, can be done in a mundane sense, or it can be a paramita if it is conjoined with bodaishin.

When done in this way, the Avatamsaka Sutra (Flower Garland Sutra) tells us, the Buddha himself could not finish describing them if he took an eon. If the qualities of a single thought of a bodhisattva who has aroused the first thought of enlightenment are deep and extensive, how much more so would it be, the sutra suggests, if they were to possess and cultivate the

4. Thera, *Devotion in Buddhism: Three Essays*, 20.

5. See Oda, "The Concept of "Faith" in the Awakening of Mahayana Faith," 9.

meritorious practices of the ten perfections and ten stages of faith outlined in the Dasabhumika Sutra (Ten Stages Sutra).

Likewise, the Lankavatara Sutra (The Sutra of the Descent to Lanka) describes how, after realizing that there is one thing which is not bound by causation, being beyond the distinction of subject and object, a person will by virtue of their faith, understand that the triple world is mind itself, and thus understanding, they will arrive at the abode of the paramitas or perfections.

In many ways, Zen built upon this practice of the mind of faith on Theravada notions of the close relation between morality, right conduct, and faith. As stated previously, to fully take refuge in the Buddha, the Dharma, the Sangha, and the precepts is to achieve pure faith so that morality arises naturally from within. In other words, faith in the Triple Gem allows the mind to purify itself. Kogen Mizuno, scholar and author, notes this of morality and faith:

> The possession of absolute faith—a faith that purifies the mind—
> and the keeping of precepts . . . are the essence of Buddhism in
> that they teach the means by which faith and morality are to be
> achieved. If faith in the three treasures is central, then the precepts
> will be followed naturally, and morality will become a function of
> faith. In the Eightfold path, right view refers to faith, while right
> speech, action, and livelihood refer to morality.[6]

In several early sutras, the Buddha mentions four qualities that lead to the superior welfare of a lay follower—faith, virtue, generosity, and wisdom. We can know when a person has faith and confidence, we are told, when they desire to see people of virtuous behavior, to hear the good Dharma, and when they have developed a mind free from miserliness. Such a person is said to be freely generous, openhanded, devoted to charity, and delights in giving and sharing.

In the Anguttara Nikaya (The Numerical Discourses) it is noted that along with faith and confidence, there comes reverence, a sense of respect and esteem. The Milinda Panha (Questions of Milinda) agrees with this observation.

> The king asked Nagasena again, "When you said just now, "by
> other good qualities," to what did you refer?" "Faith, filial obedi-
> ence, perseverance, reflection on good, meditation (samadhi),
> and wisdom are the other good qualities," said Nagasena. "What

6. Mizuno, *Essentials of Buddhism*, 174.

is faith?" then asked the king. "Faith means belief without doubt, faith in the existence of the Buddha, of the Buddha's Dharma and of the Sangha. . .If one has such faith, his mind is serene and clear and the five hindrances are eradicated. . .If people can remove all the mental evil and be faithful, clear, calm in the mind, it is just like the brilliant moon."

Unsurprisingly, in Theravada Buddhism faith is one of the five accomplishments, the other four being the accomplishment of virtues, learning, benevolence, and wisdom. In Mahayana Buddhism, the Mahaprajnaparamita Shastra (Treatise on the Perfection of Great Wisdom) tells us that as these five spiritual faculties become complete and ripen, the bodhisattva can acquire the high aspiration (adhyasaya).

The Zhengdaoge (Song of Enlightenment) states that the characteristic mark of good conduct and virtue is that it has Five *Bala* or Moral Powers as its basis. This fivefold power is gained when one has a realization which is beyond intellectual measurement. It describes the state of consciousness of the leisurely person of the Tao, the person who has clearly realized the mani-jewel of Buddha-nature.

The five powers are faith power, perseverance power, correct-thought power, samadhi power and wisdom (discernment-prajna) power. The first category, faith power, is the true faith that appears upon realizing satori. It establishes the power of conviction because once we have seen our true nature for ourselves with our own eyes, we will not be shaken in our faith.

Faith is also considered to be the power that cuts through all mistaken beliefs. These five powers are one part of the Saptatrimsadbodhi Paksikadharmah (The Thirty-seven Aids to Bodhi) which is a list, in seven parts of the attainments of a buddha. Shantideva's Sikshasamuccaya (Compendium of Precepts) gives a clear explanation of why faith itself is considered a power.

> The five faculties (of a Buddha) are Faith, Vigor, Mindfulness, Concentration and Wisdom. Here what is Faith? By this faith one has faith in four dharmas. Which four? He accepts the right view . . . puts his trust in the ripening of karma . . . has faith in the mode of life of a Bodhisattva, and . . . when in his faith he has left behind all doubts, he brings about in himself those qualities of a Buddha. This is known as the virtue of faith.[7]

The Sikshasamuccaya is not alone in pointing out that virtue equates with faith which, in turn, equates with discernment.

7. See Conze, *Buddhist Texts Through the Ages*, 185.

In the Zheng Fahua Jing, one of the six Chinese versions of the Saddharmapundarika Sutra (Lotus Sutra), the Buddha gives a teaching to Bhaisajyaraja (Medicine King Bodhisattva). He reminds Bhaisajyaraja that the Dharma is difficult to believe and awaken to. Nonetheless, if a person can uphold the teachings, then they will be endowed with the powers of great faith, of aspiration, of myriad roots of merit, and will dwell together with the Buddha.

A person thus attains these five types of vision and power through unification with the mind-essence, where they are facets of the same gem of wisdom. This implies that a moral path without faith does not have a strong foundation. As the Dasabhumika Sutra (Ten Stages Sutra) reminds us: faith is the best of vehicles, delivering us into Buddhahood. Therefore, people of intelligence rely on the guidance of faith. Virtues will not arise in people who have no faith.

As you may have guessed by now, faith is found on many of the lists that Buddhists like to compose. In the Theravada Canon faith is listed as one of the following: the three attainments and three growths, the delightful and desirable four conditions which are hard to win in the world, the four controlling powers, the five powers and five growths, the five perfecting and five treasures, the seven powers, seven treasures and seven grounds for praise, and the ten growths.[8]

The importance and versatility of faith can be summed up in the following verses from the Pali Canon. They apply to Zen faith as well.

> Faith is in this world the best property for a person; Dharma, well observed, conveys happiness; truth indeed is the sweetest of things; and that life they call the best which is lived with understanding. (Sutta Nipata (The Discourse Group) 1.10)

> The person whose associate is faith and who is full of wisdom will cut off all their bonds for the sake of attaining nirvana. (Udanavarga (Northern Buddhist Dhammapada) 10.6)

> The wise person in this world holds fast to faith and wisdom; these are their greatest treasures; they cast aside all other riches. (Udanavarga 10.9)

8. Hangthukmod, *The Importance of Saddha in Theravada Buddhism: An Analytical Study*, 61–62.

The wise person, who has real faith, morality, wisdom and who keeps them present in their mind, casts off all demeritorious actions; they are in the good way. (Udanavarga 10.7)

With faith, you cross the flood and with diligence the ocean. With effort end unpleasantness and with wisdom purify yourself. (Samyutta Nikaya 10.12)

. . . the person of intelligence, remembering the Buddha's Teaching, should be devoted to faith and virtue, to confidence and vision of the Dharma. (Samyutta Nikaya 912)

As Bhadravudha and Alavi-Gotama were delivered by faith, so you shall let faith deliver you, and you will go, O Pingiya, to the further shore of the realm of death. (Sutta Nipata 5.19)

The monastic endowed with these six things is worthy of veneration, suitable for hospitality, gifts and to honor with clasped hands, the incomparable field of merit for the world. What six? Endowed with the faculty of faith, effort, mindfulness, concentration, wisdom and destroying desires, the mind released and released through wisdom, having realized here and now he abides. (Anguttara Nikaya 6.10)

Thus, when a person recollects the faith, virtues, learnedness, benevolence, and wisdom of the gods and their own, their mind brightens up, joy arises and defilements fade. (Anguttara Nikaya 6.10)

"Not only Alara Kalama has faith, I also have faith," said the Buddha. (Majjhima Nikaya 26)

"Faith is the seed," said the Buddha, "austerities the rain, wisdom my yoke and plow, conscientiousness the pole, mind the reins, and mindfulness my driving stick." (Samyutta Nikaya 7.11)

Joy has a specific basis and is not without a specific basis. And what is the specific basis for joy? The answer should be that it is faith. (Samyutta Nikaya 12.23)

Others will be faithless; we shall be faithful here—thus effacement can be done. (Majjhima Nikaya 8)

By rising in faith and watchfulness, by self-possession and self-harmony, the wise person makes an island which water cannot overflow. (Dhammapada 25)

One who lives without looking for pleasures, their senses well controlled, moderate in food, faithful and strong, Mara will certainly not overthrow, any more than the wind throws down a rocky mountain. (Dhammapada 8)

Those who have faith in the Buddha have faith in the highest, and for those with faith in the highest, there comes the highest result. (Itivuttaka 90)

The doors of the Immortal are open. Let those who can hear respond with faith. (Digha Nikaya 18.27, Mahavagga 5.12)

Pleasant is virtue lasting to old age, pleasant is a faith firmly rooted; pleasant is the attainment of intelligence, pleasant is the avoidance of evil. (Dhammapada 333)

A lay-follower who has five qualities is a jewel of a lay-follower. . .What are these five qualities? They have faith; they are virtuous; they are not superstitious; they believe in karma and not in luck or omen. (Anguttara Nikaya 5.175)

The Mahayana Canon also has its own inventory. For example, the Dasheng Qixin Lun (The Awakening of Mahayana Faith) describes three kinds of mentality which are developed by faith. Firstly, a straightforward mentality due to direct attention to the reality of true suchness. Second, a compassionate mentality. Lastly, a profound mentality because it puts together all good conduct. (Again, it is worth noting that faith plays a pivotal role in combination with other aspects of practice.)

The Avatamsaka Sutra (Flower Garland Sutra) has a compilation of faith and its functions which reads like a list of the most important virtues in the Buddhist world.

On the long journey of human life, faith is the best of companions; it is the best refreshment on the journey; and it is the greatest possession. Faith is the hand that receives the Dharma; it is the pure hand that receives all the virtues. Faith is the fire that consumes all the impurities of worldly desires, it removes the burden, and it is the guide that leads one's way. Faith removes greed, fear, and pride; it teaches courtesy and to respect others; it frees one from the bondage of circumstances; it gives one courage to meet hardship; it gives one power to overcome temptations; it enables one to keep one's deeds bright and pure; and it enriches the mind with wisdom. Faith is the encouragement when one's way is long and wearisome, and it leads to Enlightenment. Faith makes us feel that we are in the presence of Buddha and it brings us to where Buddha's arm supports us. Faith softens our hard and selfish minds and gives us a friendly spirit and a mind of understanding sympathy.[9]

In Zen faith is so instrumental that it is one of its three pillars of Zen along with great doubt and great courage.

Hakuin explained the pivotal role of doubt, courage, and faith in Zen practice. He drew attention to the fact that the practice of Zen requires three essentials: a great root of faith, a feeling of great doubt, and a great, burning aspiration. If we lack any one of these, he said, we are like a three-legged cauldron with one leg broken off.

In his Chanshi Chanyao (Three Essentials of Chan) Gaofeng Yuanmiao explained that if we are thinking of making a genuine and realistic investigation of Zen, we absolutely must employ these three great attitudes for enlightenment to occur. Great faith (sometimes called great trust or confidence), great doubt and great determination (sometimes called great resolve or courage) are necessary for great death, the non-attachment to the separate self.

In previous chapters we looked at great faith. To understand what we mean by great doubt, however, we need to distinguish it from the common garden variety of doubt, skepticism or unsurety. Ordinary doubt is known in Buddhism as one of the five hindrances to effective practice. The other four consist of sensory desire (seeking happiness through the five senses of sight, sound, smell, taste, and physical feeling), ill-will, sloth-torpor, and restlessness-worry (the inability to calm the mind). These five delusive inclinations constitute the most fundamental of illusions or earthly desires.

Ordinary doubt demonstrates a lack of conviction or trust in the Triple Gem and the efficaciousness of the Dharma. It also refers to inner doubts about our own ability to understand and implement the Dharma. Linji warned that when we have one thought of doubt, instantly Mara enters our mind. If we want to fully embody the Dharma, he advised, just have no doubts. Linji saw non-thinking as the antidote since its foundation is faith in one's true mind and its activity.

9. Bukkyo Dendo Kyokai, *The Teaching of Buddha*, 179–80.

The Visuddhimagga (The Path of Purification) notes that uncertainty is characterized by doubt. Its function is to waver, and it is manifested as a lack of motivation and ambiguity. Its proximate or close cause is unwise attention, and it should be seen as a hindrance to practice. The Buddha himself said that he knew of no other single thing that has the power to bring on doubt and to cause doubt to increase than unwise attention.

This kind of doubt is not the great doubt of Zen, especially as its effects are negative and it is something to be eliminated or abandoned. Zen's great doubt (*daigidan*) is the opposite of this. Zen takes doubt and uses it to find the truth. Dahui taught that all doubts are in fact one doubt—the doubt about the truth. If we focus all our attention on that one great doubt, then all doubts will be in that instant destroyed through realization. Thus, our enlightenment will be in proportion to our doubt. A common maxim in Zen Buddhism is "great doubt, great awakening; small doubt, small awakening; no doubt, no awakening."

This can be difficult for some of us to get our head around since religious doubt in the Judeo-Christian tradition is sometimes viewed as shameful. There has been a long history of opposition between faith and doubt in the Christian tradition with each of them occupying opposite ends of a spectrum. Consequently, some of us might feel that if we have doubts, it means that we are denying the teachings or that we have failed to foster doubtless faith. If we keep in mind, however, that Zen faith is not absolute faith but perfect faith which encourages questioning, then we can see that doubt is not necessarily a bad thing.

Great doubt does not indicate a lack of trust in the teachings but deep existential doubt about the very nature of reality. Our great faith tells us that everything is perfect and lacking nothing, and yet we experience the opposite in our daily life. Great doubt and great faith are two aspects of bodaishin. Torei suggested that there is a particular relationship between them. He suggested that we should know that true realization is just great doubt amid great faith. That is, we can't know them as separated. When the time comes, realization will naturally manifest itself. As Dahui noted, beneath great doubt there is always a great awakening.

According to Yuanmiao, faith is not only the catalyst for realization it is a beneficial influence constantly emanating from our enlightened nature, prompting all conscious beings toward enlightenment. Since we cover our innate nature with delusion, however, Yuanmiao felt that the perfection of faith alone cannot be a sufficient prerequisite to enlightenment.

Rather, the natural tension between faith and doubt serves as the catalyst for the experience of awakening. Yuanmiao viewed both as symbiotic so that the more faith we have, the more doubt we have too. In a formula similar to that of the Dasheng Qixin Lun (The Awakening of Mahayana Faith), his Essentials of Zen describes faith as the essence of doubt, while awakening is the function of doubt.

Basically, then, Yuanmiao believed that religious doubt arises from deep faith. The tension between them creates an existential quandary that ultimately leads to the experience of awakening. Great faith is the affirmation of emptiness and buddha nature whereas great doubt represents the negation of the self. So, in a sense, awakening is not to be rid of doubt but to use it to get to a state which transcends the duality of faith and doubt. To persist with a koan, for example, and then experience a breakthrough realization is to realize the non-duality of faith and doubt.

The task then is to go beyond that momentary event and integrate non-duality permanently into our daily life. Using the tension between doubt and faith, we continue to use both as fuel for spiritual growth. As Torei suggested, having both doubt and faith ensures progress on the Way.

This is because great doubt is the mechanism by which we propel ourselves out of the self, and it is the conviction of great faith which holds us steady on the path. Without the nourishment of faith, doubt can descend into skepticism, frustration, and humiliation, and without doubt, faith is blind belief. Strong doubt exists in proportion to strong faith. These two provide the dynamic tension of the enlightenment journey.

It goes without saying, therefore, that we also need a large amount of determination to keep going. Great determination or courage (*daifunshi*) is not just ordinary effort with a large dose of energy thrown in for good measure. It is an overwhelming determination to dispel great doubt. That is, we simply cannot rest until we know the true self.

Dahui said that if we want to transcend birth and death and cross the sea of suffering, we must raise straight the banner of effort. Directly beneath it, faith will become sufficient. Only when this faith has become sufficient, he believed, will enlightenment take place. As the Dasheng Qixin Lun (The Awakening of Mahayana Faith) points out, for sentient beings who pursue practice with courage and vigor, attainment of buddhahood can take place in a single moment of thought.

Daifunshi is also known as great indignant will because the Sino-Japanese characters for this word suggest indignance at the fact that we have not yet totally exerted ourselves to reach our goal. Yamada taught that indignant means that we become insistent with ourselves. We want to know why everyone else has come to realization but not us.

So, we get exasperated with ourselves, he says, and give the *kyosaku*[10] to ourselves before we receive it from someone else. In other words, dai-funshi is a desperate conviction to overcome all impediments. We become a "lump of doubt" so that our entire being becomes focused on fully realizing the answer until the question sticks in our throats like "a red-hot iron ball." It is an intense desire to know the truth. To clarify the great matter, we exercise every bit of our perseverance and, as Hakuin would say, thrust forth the courageous mind derived from faith.

Faith and the other practices and virtues that it is associated with together form a holistic approach to life. Faith is not a minor element of the Dharma but intrinsic to understanding not only Zen but attaining realization as well. Numerous sutras and teachers tell us that when we embody great faith, doubt and determination, our body and mind, indeed the whole universe, becomes a buddha-field or a pure land in which ultimate separation does not exist. This aspect is not limited to Zen but is found within Pure Land and Nichiren as well. How they employ the doctrine of a pure land and enlightenment within it will be the topic of our last discussion of faith.

10. The kyosaku is known as the Encouragement Stick, a wooden stick or slat used during periods of meditation to remedy sleepiness or lapses of concentration.

9

Faith As A Bridge

At times Buddhists in the West have let certain preconceptions get in the way of establishing a working connection with faith-based traditions. Instead, they have often been dismissed for their faith emphasis or assumed lack of efficacy. Writing in the late 1920s, British historian Sir Charles Eliot even went so far as to ask whether Japanese Pure Land should be referred to as "Buddhism" at all.

To a great degree, that sentiment still stands true today. As a *Tricycle: The Buddhist Review* article noted, it is not an exaggeration to say that, for many of its readers, approaches to Buddhism that are not based on a practice of quiet, focused sitting meditation are, other than in name, scarcely recognizable as Buddhist at all.

Yet, as Yin Kuang, Thirteenth Ancestor of Pure Land points out, although Pure Land Buddhism has different practices to Zen, it still concerns suffering and the liberation from suffering. In the Preface to *Pure-Land Zen, Zen Pure-Land: Letters from Patriarch Yin Kuang* he writes:

> After the demise of the historical Buddha, his teachings. . . developed into ten different schools, several of which remain important to this day: Zen, Tantric and Pure Land . . . All these schools teach the same basic truth: "Do not what is evil, do what is good, keep the mind pure." True to this spirit, the Pure Land approach is simple and straightforward.
>
> Through *mindfulness of the Buddha* (i.e., Buddha Recitation), the practitioner can calm his mind and achieve samadhi and wisdom.

> Thus reborn in the Pure Land (i.e., in his pure Mind), he will eventually attain Buddhahood. This is also the core teaching, the very essence, of Zen and all other Mahayana schools. As D.T. Suzuki has pointed out, "the psychological effects of the repetition of the holy name are close to the effects of Zen meditation."[1]

So, while Zen and faith-based traditions are in many ways not the same, we do not have to leave or compromise our tradition to form a bridge. This is not to say that we should view other practices through Zen lenses, but that we understand and acknowledge that in their own way, each tradition seeks the same thing—to leave the confines of the separate-self and achieve liberation.

Zen practitioners can also see other practices through the common denominator of faith and appreciate to a greater degree what our fellow Buddhists of different traditions do because we too have practices and notions that serve similar (but not always the same) functions. Using an informed understanding of faith as a common point, we can come to a greater understanding of the big picture. In other words, we can appreciate the role of faith in other traditions because we see the value and efficacy of it in our own.

In doing this, we can improve our knowledge of not only other Buddhist traditions but Zen as well. To this end, I have chosen some useful examples to illustrate this. Hopefully, these can show that there are many connection points for Zennists to recognize that faith-based practices and thought are as varied, interesting, and efficacious as Zen ones. I will take two faith-based traditions, the Pure Land and Nichiren schools, as examples.

Nichiren Buddhism is a branch of Mahayana Buddhism based on the teachings of the thirteenth-century Japanese monk Nichiren Shonin and is a comprehensive term covering several major schools and sub-schools which are based upon the conviction that the true teachings of the Buddha can be found only in the Saddharmapundarika Sutra (Lotus Sutra).

The sutra is one of the most popular and important texts in Mahayana Buddhism and is the central text used by the Tientai and Nichiren sects. Influential in the lives of at least three Zen masters (Hakuin, Huineng, and Dogen), it is also important in Zen, with Dogen referring to it as the "Sutra of Sutras." It is considered a complete representation of the heart and culmination of the Buddha's teaching.

---

1. Kuang, *Pure-Land Zen, Zen Pure-Land: Letters from Patriarch Yin Kuang,* 5.

Pure Land Buddhism comprises the schools of Buddhism that stress faith in a particular buddha, Amida, to achieve Buddhahood. The Sukhavativyuha Sutra (Infinite Life Sutra) teaches that by the power of Amida's fundamental vow to save sentient beings, those who hear and recite his name, rejoice in faith, and wish to be reborn, will all reach his celestial abode or Pure Land. They will all naturally attain a state of non-retrogression.

Shandao Dashi, an influential seventh-century Buddhist prominent in China, Korea, Vietnam, and Japan, wrote that five activities lead to rebirth in this Western Paradise: uttering the name of the Buddha, chanting the sutras, meditating on the Buddha, and revering and singing praises to the Buddha. Hua-yen and Zen master Tsung-mi categorized Pure Land practices as consisting of vocal invocation of the Buddha's name, concentration on a physical representation of the Buddha, mental visualization of the Buddha, and identification of the self with Amida Buddha.[2] This is not surprising considering that the Japanese term nembutsu derives from the Sanskrit *buddhanusmrti*, which means to think about the Buddha and to keep the Buddha in mind through recitation and visualization.

While Nichiren Buddhism focuses on one sutra, three major sutras play an important part in the Pure Land tradition. These are the Longer Sukhavativyuha Sutra (Infinite Life Sutra), the Shorter Sukhavativyuha Sutra (Amitabha Sutra), and the Amitayurdhyana Sutra (Sutra of Immeasurable Life as Told by the Buddha). All these concern Amida, his compassionate vows, and the nature of his pure land.

A commonplace distinction has often been made between two camps of Pure Land perception and practice, depending on the background and the capacities of the cultivator. Firstly, at the popular level, historically there have always been those who pray to Amida to be reborn in the best conditions for practice i.e., in the Pure Land. In the celestial abode of the Pure Land, there is none of the suffering, defilement, and delusion that normally hinders our efforts toward enlightenment here in this *saha* or suffering world. This means that the Pure Land is an ideal training ground where a practitioner is reborn through complete faith (shinjin) and the power of Amida's vows to save all who call his name.

Secondly, as with any branch of Buddhism, Buddhahood is attained by overcoming the ignorance of the ordinary, deluded mind through the development of the wisdom of the true mind. In *Heart of the Shin Buddhist Path: A Life of Awakening*, Takamaro Shigaraki, a Japanese Buddhist philosopher

2. Baroni, *Obaku Zen: The Emergence of the Third Sect of Zen*, 110.

and Jodo Shinshu (New Pure Land) priest, explains this further. He points out that while in the Sanskrit version of the Longer Sukhavativyuha Sutra (Infinite Life Sutra), the word *prasada-citta* denotes entrusting (*shin-jiru*) in Amida Buddha, it has also been translated as *shojo* or *chojo* (purity), *joshin* (pure trust), *shingyo* (entrusting with joy), and shinjin.

> Entrusting in Amida Buddha thus refers to a state of mind . . . in which one's heart and mind become pure and serene, giving rise to great joy. This form of *shin* is completely non-dualistic and subjective in nature. It does not imply that we must do something vis-à-vis some object. Shinjin is equivalent to the state of *samādhi* in which one visualizes the Buddha. It points to the experience of awakening, whereby one directly encounters the Buddha. Shinjin is identical with true insight, or literally, "knowing and seeing."[3]

This can be achieved within one lifetime through the practice of Buddha Recitation—reciting the nembutsu.

Thich Thien Tam, author of *Buddhism of Wisdom and Faith: Pure Land Principles and Practice* explains how this works:

> If we have the roots and the temperament of Mahayana followers, we should naturally understand that the goal of Buddha Recitation is to achieve Buddhahood . . . as we begin reciting, the past, present and future have lost their distinction, marks exist but they have been left behind, form is emptiness, thought is the same as No-Thought, the realm of the Original Nature "apart from thought" of the Tathagata has been penetrated. This state is Buddhahood; what else could it be?[4]

Rebirth thus occurs in the practitioner themselves. In this mind-only Pure Land, Amida, the Buddha of Infinite Light and Life, is synonymous with buddha nature, luminous and perpetual. According to this perspective, therefore, the Pure Land is the mind. As the Longer Sukhavativyuha Sutra (Infinite Life Sutra) states, Amida Buddha is not far from anyone.

The sutra goes on to say that while his Land of Purity is far away to the West it is also within the minds of those who earnestly wish to be with him. To those who have faith, it reminds us, Amida offers the opportunity to become one with him. Since Amida is the all-inclusive body of equality, whenever someone thinks of Amida, Amida thinks of him and enters his

---

3. Shigaraki, *Heart of the Shin Buddhist Path*, 68–70.

4. Tam, *Buddhism of Wisdom and Faith*, 79.

mind freely. Thus, when a person thinks of Buddha, he has Buddha's mind in all its pure, happy and peaceful perfection.

The Amitayur-Dhyana Sutra (The Sutra of Visualizing the Buddha of Infinite Life and Light) explores the implications of this. It states that since all buddhas are the dharma-realm, when we think of the Buddha, our very mind is, in essence, identical to the thirty-two major and eighty minor marks of the Buddha. Moreover, since the mind produces the Buddha, it is axiomatic that outside of mind there is no Buddha.

This means that the success or failure of an individual's practice depends on his depth of faith and understanding, that is, on his heart-mind. Consider this statement from Yanshou which emphasizes the identity of the one mind in which all phenomena are but the product of consciousness. This is the state where principle and activity are not in dualism.

> Know that if you become conscious of mind, you will be born into the Pure Land that is naught but mind, but if you are attached to external objects, you will fall into the midst of those objects with which you associate. If you are clear that there is no difference between cause and effect, you will understand that there is no dharma apart from mind.[5]

This expresses the notion that the Pure Land is the original purity of one's own mind.

At the end of his life, when a disciple asked Honen Shonin, founder of the first independent branch of Japanese Pure Land, if he would be born in the Pure Land, he replied, "Since I have always been in the Pure Land, that will not happen." From this perspective, the Pure Land is not some place where we go but buddhahood itself.

It is for this reason that the Pure Land is known as *hodo*, a requited land. Shoto Hase in *The Eastern Buddhist* journal explains the significance of this:

> That the Pure Land is a requited land means that it is not an other-worldly place which exists somewhere objectively, but instead is a place where the immeasurable life of the Tathagata is bestowed upon us as nourishment. A place where we live off the life of Amida Buddha is called a requited land. "Faith" refers to none other than attesting to the action of immeasurable life functioning within ourselves as the energy by which we live . . . eternal life is . . . a point that might be called "nothingness-as-love." The Pure

5. Sharf, "On Pure Land Buddhism and Ch'an," 315.

Land concept of the original vow arose from the intuition of this truth.[6]

In other words, the egolessness of the arising of faith, that is, the purity of the mind-ground, directly results in rebirth in the mind-only Pure Land.

Jichihan, a late Heian era monk of the Himitsu Nembutsu tradition (the esoteric nembutsu of the Shingon (True Word) School explicitly pointed out that Amida is immanent in the mind and body of the practitioner; that the Pure Land is not separate from our present reality. His Byochu Shugyo Ki (Notes on Practice During Illness) emphasizes the non-duality of Amida and the practitioner. Since Amida exists in one's own body, the Land of Bliss is right here. It encourages us to realize that oneself and Amida are non-dual.

According to T'an-luan, the Third Ancestor in Jodo Shinshu Buddhism, this means that since the Pure Land is none other than the dharma-body that is everywhere equal, the one-pointed samadhi of faith enables us to instantly manifest in innumerable universes, making offerings to the buddhas of the ten directions without ever moving from the Pure Land. In other words, samsara and nirvana carry the same ontological status—samsara is nirvana and nirvana, samsara. The Pure Land is in fact, samsara viewed through awakened eyes.

Likewise, Yanshou, a supporter of syncretic Pure Land-Zen practice, considered nembustu practice as just one of multitude ways to the awaken to emptiness, and that to attain birth in the Pure Land of mind is also to fulfill the bodhisattva vows. This is because a reborn person is an awakened person who, as a matter of course, "returns" to the samsaric, ordinary world in an awakened state to save suffering beings. While there have been many in Zen's history who disagreed with Pure Land practice (Hakuin was especially critical), it is easy to see that this second form lends itself to the Zen notion of mutual identity and interpenetration.

Zen practitioners might also connect with it through Huineng's statements in the Liuzu Tan Jing (Platform Sutra). While he too was critical of the concept of a Pure Land in another realm, Huineng nevertheless drew attention to the fact that if the mind gives rise to impurities, even though we invoke the Buddha and seek to be reborn in the Western Paradise, it will be difficult to reach there. Instead, when the mind is pure, the buddha-land is pure, and without false thoughts, every place is the land of ultimate bliss.

6. Hase and Conway, "Faith and Inochi as Infinite Life," 279, 291.

This is also the sentiment of Vimalakirti in the Vimalakirti Nirdesa Sutra (The Sutra Spoken by the Layman Vimalakirti). He taught that if we want to go to the Pure Land, then we must purify our mind. When the mind (and faith) is pure, then whatever we see will be pure and wherever we go we will find the buddha realm.

The Pratyutpanna Samadhi Sutra (Sutra of the Samadhi of Being in the Presence of All Buddhas) outlines how this process works.

> Bodhisattvas hear about the Buddha Amitabha and call him to mind again and again in this land. Because of this calling to mind, they see the Buddha Amitabha. Having seen him they ask him what dharmas it takes to be born in the realm of the Buddha Amitabha. Then the Buddha Amitabha says to these bodhisattvas: "If you wish to come and be born in my realm, you must always call me to mind again and again, you must always keep this thought in mind without letting up, and thus you will succeed in coming to be born in my realm."[7]

This aspect of Pure Land Buddhahood is perhaps the easiest for Zen practitioners to understand, even though the Zen school has sometimes voiced strong disapproval of recitation as a way of completely embodying faith.

Yet as Jinshu pointed out in the Kuan-hsin Lun (Treatise on the Contemplation of the Mind), recitation is not merely a technique or the empty repetition of a buddha's name, it can be true contemplation.

> "Buddha" means "awakening." This means to awaken and penetrate the source of mind and not allow evil to arise. "Contemplation" means "reflect upon." This is to firmly maintain the practice of morality and not to forget to diligently seek to understand the Tathagata's teaching. This is called "correct contemplation." Therefore, understand that contemplation resides in the mind, not in words . . . You use words to get at the meaning, and when you have grasped the meaning you can forget about the words. To praise contemplation of the Buddha is to say that one must practice the very essence of contemplation of the Buddha. If the mind is not true, one's utterances will be empty and one's contemplation will be wasted effort.[8]

---

7. *The Pratyutpanna Samadhi Sutra and the Surangama Samadhi Sutra*, 2–3, 19.

8. Sharf, *The Treasure Store Treatise (Pao-tsang lun)*, 106.

In his Dasabhumika Sutra (Ten Stages Sutra), Nagarjuna explains that the stage of non-retrogression is attainable by visualizing a buddha or by hearing a buddha's name.

Agreeing with this, Xuyun taught that all expedient methods taught by the Buddha are good for treating worldly illnesses, and the recitation of the Buddha's name is an *agada* (medicine) that cures all diseases. However, all methods require a firm faith, inflexible resolution, and considerable practice to give good results. If you are strong in faith, Xuyun observed, you will achieve the same perfection whether you concentrate on mantras, practice Zen, or repeat the Buddha's name.

Moreover, as the late Sheng-Yen in his book *Hoofprint of the Ox—Principles of the Chan Buddhist Path* pointed out, the technique of reciting the names of buddhas and bodhisattvas is as old as the practice of Buddha-mindfulness itself. In East Asian circles, he states, Zen Buddhists have often used the practice of Buddha-mindfulness and meditation on Amida Buddha or the bodhisattva *Avalokitesvara* (*Guanyin/Kannon*) to direct their attention toward the realization of buddha nature within. Thus, in Zen there is a saying "Amida is our original nature, and the Pure Land is none other than the mind." Both Zen and Pure Land practitioners put their whole being into recitation so that they may achieve a state of single-minded concentration without confusion.

As I stated in chapter 3, syncretic Pure Land-Zen practice came to be considered by Chinese practitioners as a natural and legitimate combination. In the Chixiu Baizhang Qinggui (The Baizhang Zen Monastic Regulations), for example, chanting the nembutsu at funerals was listed as standard practice. Throughout the history of Zen in China there have been teachers who have recognized the efficacy of both methods.

Yanshou, for example, made prominent use of the nembutsu within Zen training. He formulated the Ssu Lia Chien (Fourfold Summary of Zen and Pure Land) which outlines a concise formula for the combination of the two practices.

> With Ch'an but no Pure Land, nine out of ten people will go astray. When death comes suddenly, they must accept it in an instant. With Pure Land but no Ch'an, ten thousand out of ten thousand people will achieve birth [in the Pure Land]. If one can see Amitabha face to face, why worry about not attaining awakening? With both Ch'an and Pure Land, it is like a tiger who has grown horns. One will be a teacher for mankind in this life, and a Buddhist patriarch in the next. With neither Ch'an nor Pure Land, it

is like falling on an iron bed with bronze posters [i.e., one of the hells]. For endless kalpas one will find nothing to rely on."[9]

Another Zen master, Zhiche Duanyun, came to his awakening through the nembutsu *koan* of "The one doing this nembutsu—who is it?" This nembutsu practice was so valued in China that Zhongfeng Mingben, a prominent Yuan-period monk who greatly contributed to the Chan/Pure Land synthesis, is known to have said "Chan is the Chan of the Pure Land and the Pure Land is the Pure Land of Chan"[10]

Konggu Jinglong, a lineage descendant of Gaofeng Yuanmiao, described the nembutsu as the most important shortcut method of training. Hanshan Deqing, one of the great masters of the Ming period, taught that the single practice of the nembutsu is the true huatou (head word or critical phrase of a koan), the supremely easy method of gaining succor in this world of dust.[11]

Contemporary Japanese teacher, Kosho Uchiyama, author of the seminal *Opening the Hand of Thought*, framed buddha recitation in this way for a Zen audience: "When people of the Pure Land school chant namu amida butsu, they are doing zazen with their mouths, and when we do zazen, we are performing namu amida butsu with our whole body."[12]

The late Reverend Master Jiyu-Kennett of the Order of Buddhist Contemplatives believed there is room in the world for both viewpoints, for Zen and "the devotional, pietistic and the intuitive." Despite having heard it said by some that Pure Land and Zen were incompatible, both she and her teacher, the Very Reverend Keido Chisan Koho Zenji, Abbot of Sojiji, concluded that although externally these entrances to the Dharma might seem to be very different, it is impossible to say definitively which entrance to the Dharma is the right one to enter for they are not separate, and the way in which one starts training can only be decided by the individual concerned.

As for the Nichiren school, Nichiren Shonin also exhorted his followers to strengthen their faith and receive the protection of Shakyamuni and the buddhas of the ten directions. Chant namu myoho renge kyo, he advised, as a person lays down their life for their partner or as parents refuse to abandon their children.

9. Heng-ching, "Yung-ming's Syncretism of Pure Land and Ch'an," 118.

10. Zhang, *A Study of Chinese Buddhism: Focusing on Zhixu*, 386.

11. Furuta, *Zen and the Pure Land*, 23.

12. Uchiyama, *Opening the Hand of Thought*, 87.

Daniel Montgomery, Saddharmapundarika Sutra (Lotus Sutra) scholar, explains that in namu myoho renge kyo we identify with the Buddha. In namu myoho renge kyo the Buddha identifies with us. This identification is complete in every respect. Just as the Buddha is three bodies in one, so are we. The person who chants namu myoho renge kyo, therefore, is a Buddha. Their body is the dharma-body of the Buddha, their mind, the reward-body of the Buddha and their behavior, the manifestation-body of the Buddha.

This does not involve "transforming" oneself into a buddha. The Cosmic Buddha of the Saddharmapundarika Sutra (Lotus Sutra) teaches that we can become a buddha at once without any transformation when we identify with the essential. This was role-modeled by Shakyamuni when he completely identified himself with the dharmakaya. Consequently, ordinary people are themselves the Buddha when they single-mindedly chant with strong faith. This is how we attain enlightenment without the rigorous training of a monk.

This brings in another way that Zen Buddhists might connect with Pure Land Buddhism, that is, the recognition that there is a certain similar cadence to the practice of Dogen and Shinran Shonin, founder of the Pure Land school in Japan—they both based their practices on the fact of buddha nature or intrinsic enlightenment. Both Dogen and Shinran rejected the notion of acquiring something from practice since practice was the expression of an already present buddha nature.

For Dogen this understanding manifested itself in just sitting—a meditative practice which is not the means to achieve enlightenment but the natural expression or function of it. For Shinran, the nembutsu was an expression of the fact that we are already equal to the Buddhas. While his nembutsu is popularly but incorrectly perceived as "just" devotional, it has always been more than that. It is the total meditative or contemplative embodiment of entrusting-mind.

Instead of being a practice, therefore, Shinran's nembutsu is the expression of *tathata* or suchness itself. It is not said to achieve or acquire anything but instead, is simply how Amida is expressed through a particular person. It is said purely because we have already attained liberation, that is, birth in the Pure Land. Consequently, Shinran equates shinjin, entrusting mind, to buddha nature which in turn is equivalent to the Tathagata itself in much the same way that Dogen equates shikantaza with buddha nature.

This also stands true for other meditative kinds of nembutsu practiced throughout Japanese Buddhist history. *Jogyo zanmai* or constantly walking, for example, was a form of meditative nembutsu employed by the Tendai school which combined reciting the name of Amida with walking meditation. A person walked round a statue of Amida reciting his name and visualizing him so that they would realize the non-duality of buddha and the practitioner.

Genshin, the most influential of several Tendai scholars active during the tenth and eleventh centuries in Japan, popularized contemplative nembutsu (*kan nembutsu*). This also involved samadhi practice through visualization and devotional or emotive practices.

Historically, Shingon Buddhism has also combined nembutsu practice with an awareness of innate presence. In this esoteric school, phenomena are not distinct from Dainichi, the Japanese version of *Vairocana*, one of the Five Primordial Buddhas considered the dharma body of the historical buddha. As such, any sound is Dainichi's voice and any thing is co-existent with the buddha's body, the dharmakaya. Their secret nembutsu rejects the nembutsu as mere recitation. Rather, it is identified with the breath or life force, so that just breathing or voicing something becomes the breathing of the nembutsu itself.[13]

Zen practitioners might also use the two truths to relate to faith-based Buddhism. I mentioned previously that in the Dasheng Qixin Lun (The Awakening of Mahayana Faith), the one mind has two aspects—the suchness aspect and the arising-ceasing aspect—and that for a properly balanced practice both must be recognized. Zen does this through faith in becoming a buddha and faith as Buddha.

This relationship between the phenomenal and essential is also expressed in the two Pure land approaches to liberation. Consider these words from Yuanjue Yuanxian:

> There are two aspects with regard to the faith in the Buddha's words. One is faith in the principle; the other is faith in the phenomenal. Faith in the principle means to believe that one's mind is the Pure Land and one's nature is the Buddha Amitabha. Faith in the phenomenal means to believe that the Pure Land lies in the Western Region, and that Buddha Amitabha resides there . . . These two aspects of faith are both one and two, yet neither one nor two. To have faith in this manner is called true faith.[14]

13. Grumbach, "Nenbutsu and Meditation," 93, 96, 98–99.
14. Sharf, *The Treasure Store Treatise*, 113.

Here we can see that these two aspects of Pure Land Buddhism are representative of the subjective and objective or popular and mind-only approaches. Thus, there is a dialectic between one's own heart and mind, and the heart and mind of Amida Buddha, having both a dichotomous identity and a non-dichotomous relationship.[15]

In a manner strikingly like Dogen's burning question of why we have to practice when we are already enlightened, the Longshu Zengguang Jingtu Wen (Awakening of Faith in the Pure Land) uses these two truths of the Pure Land to explain practice.

> . . . the Western Pure Land has (a difference between) principle and traces. In reference to the principle . . . to say that only the mind is the Pure Land and that there is no other Pure Land, and that as your own nature is Amitabha, there is no necessity to further meet with Amitabha, is wrong. Furthermore, to believe that there is a Pure Land, and to flounder in the theory of 'mind-only' and think there is no need to be reborn in the Western land, and to think that if you investigate Chan, you are enlightened to your nature and transcend the buddhas and patriarchs and that there is no need to meet Amitabha is completely mistaken.[16]

There are other related sets of terms that also characterize these two facets of Pure Land such as form and formless, mythological and demythological, celestial and psychological, futuristic, and present, transcendent, and immanent, phenomenal and noumenal, prescriptive and descriptive, poetic and philosophical, ontic and epistemological, and hypostatized and non-substantial.[17]

Again, since Zen practitioners are familiar in their own way with the notion of phenomenal and essential, they can appreciate the above descriptions. Essentially, then, Pure Land Buddhism is a religion both of faith in Amida Buddha and in our capacity to achieve Buddhahood in the here and now.

In fact, Pure Land can be a timely reminder that Zen is also saving, a fact which is not often on the radar of Western practitioners. To some of us in the western Zen world, Zen is akin to a kind of psychic hygiene, a way of trying to feel calmer, wiser, more compassionate, or enlightened. These often-subconscious curative fantasies about spiritual practice are based on

15. See Sugiyama, "The Essence of Shinran's Teaching," 300.

16. Jorgenson, *Hyujeong: Selected Works*, 123–24.

17. Tanaka, "Where is the Pure Land?," 36.

the illusion that we can somehow fix all the things about ourselves that we imagine are bad or wrong or unacceptable.

In the modern western appropriation of Zen Buddhism, Zen has often been viewed as a spiritual exercise designed to achieve higher states of personal consciousness or restorative calm. Contrary to present conventions, however, Zen Buddhism developed and cannot be fully understood outside of a worldview that sees reality itself as a vital, ephemeral agent of awareness and healing.[18] As liberation itself, it has always been more than a set of techniques, a mental ideal or a therapeutic tool.

Pure Land and its emphasis upon salvation also remind us of this fact. Some of us might shy away from the term salvation due to its Judeo-Christian associations. It is certainly true that in Buddhism there is no self to save and for this reason, Zen has never focused on salvation as such. Nevertheless, Zen and Zen faith do in a sense save us from the confines of the separate self and open us up to Hakuin's "boundless sky of samadhi."

The notion that the Pure Land is not some place where we go but buddhahood itself also gives us a particular presentation of Buddha as the dharmakaya. In Mahayana Buddhism the dharmakaya is the permanent, undifferentiated, comprehending truth. Yet, as I explained previously, this does not mean that it does not actively respond to the practitioner. Rather, as Case 52 of the Shoyoroku (Book of Serenity) tells us, it manifests form in response to beings as the mind of faith penetrates the buddhas and bodhisattvas and causes them to respond.

D. T. Suzuki viewed the dharmakaya as possessing innumerable merits and virtues and an absolute perfect intelligence which makes it an inexhaustible fountainhead of love and compassion. Thus, myoshu (incomprehensible assistance) is the ever-present compassion that functions in emptiness and which guarantees kanno doko (mutually illuminating co-experience).

So important is kanno doko, that Guifeng Zonghmi employed it in his account of Zen ancestral succession. Indeed, Dogen's teacher, Tiantong Rujing, taught that if there were no mystical communion, that is, kanno doko, the buddhas wouldn't have appeared in the world and Bodhidharma wouldn't have come from the West. Dainin Katagiri explains how this works:

> The spiritual communion between the Buddha and the practicer,
> the Buddha and you, is the interacting communion of appeal and
> response . . . Then, the response comes from the whole universe. If

18. Leighton, *Visions of Awakening Space and Time*, 3.

> we feel this spirit of the universe completely and appeal for help, or
> appeal that we may come alive in our everyday life, very naturally,
> we can be one with the universe. This is response.[19]

This active sense of the dharmakaya is also present in Pure Land Buddhism which equates Amida Buddha with the life that connects all things. He is an active, liberating force who personifies the power to release ordinary people from samsara and to bring love and compassion into the world. To Pure Land Buddhists, this is the nature of reality. The name Amida literally means without measure and Amida Buddha represents infinite time and space or the presence of Buddha in the world for all time.

The Amida who thus appears to the buddha-recitation practitioner, as well as the Amida who manifests to the Pure Land devotee at death, are both active manifestations of the dharmakaya. According to Shinran, Amida Buddha is none other than the Dharma-body as suchness which is formless and cannot be grasped. Hence, Amida is another name for the ultimate, which in this case, is given the name of a buddha.

Interestingly, while Japanese Pure Land made faith the prime method for rebirth in the Pure Land, Chinese Pure Land saw Amida's active power in the form of *ganying* (or kanying) as the key to buddhahood. Ganying means the correlative resonance pulsating throughout the field of energy that infuses the cosmos.

Chinese Buddhism explicitly identifies the mechanism of spiritual empowerment with ganying. It teaches that since ganying is the principle underlying the interaction between practitioner and buddha (in this case, the dharmakaya), a person is said to stimulate or affect the buddha, an action that elicits a compassionate response.

Jizang, the founder of Chinese Madhyamika, taught that stimulus-response is the great tenet of the buddha-dharma, the essential teaching of the many sutras. Since all sentient beings possess the seeds of goodness, he argued, they can induce the buddhas to descend and take shape in front of them, and the buddhas will meet them in welcome.[20] This is reflected, for example, in Shingon Buddhism's expression "affect the buddha."

Accordingly, the mind of faith is the Tathagata transforming itself and appearing within sentient beings or what Pure Land practitioners would call "the realization of the merit transference of the pure mind of the vow" made by the Tathagata. This is described clearly and eloquently by Shoto Hase:

19. Katagiri, *Returning To Silence: Zen Practice in Daily Life,* 83.

20. Sharf, *Coming to Terms with Chinese Buddhism,* 122.

> The Tathagata changing form and manifesting itself in sentient beings is called merit transference. Faith is the expression of the Tathagata's mind of merit transference within sentient beings. As something that calls on sentient beings drawing them to the country of the Tathagata, it is the aspect of merit transference for going forth toward the Pure Land, while as the working that calls out to sentient beings, it is the returning aspect of merit transference.[21]

As we recite the name of Amida we put our mind in tune so to speak, with Amida's. Yamada once said that the practice of Zen is to forget the self in the act of uniting with something. In Pure Land Buddhism, the separate self is embraced by the immeasurable and boundless Amida Buddha.

When we are grasped by Amida, Shinran commented, immediately we become established in the stage of the "truly settled." This is not so much an act of belief as surrender or acceptance of Amida's compassion. To chant namu amida butsu is to receive compassion from Amida, not out of our own intent but Amida's. So, for the nembutsu to be great practice given to us by Amida and not recitation through our own will, Pure Land followers believe they must totally chant as the entrustment of the primal vow of Amida itself. We must enter the ocean of the vow so that Amida's mind and ours become one.

As Shinran said, to hear the vow of Amida and be completely without doubt is the one moment of shinjin. In this way, the entrusting mind of the adherent becomes Amida's own trustworthy mind. This is described as a joyful trust (*shingyo*) and is synonymous with seeing Amida's face at the time of death. A Zen person might connect with this if they have experienced the "joyous recollection" of suchness of the person of faith outlined in the Dasheng Qixin Lun (The Awakening of Mahayana Faith).

To fully enact Pure Land practice, therefore, the unification of the cognizing subject with the cognized object must occur. This happens the moment a person's entrustment becomes settled i.e., when they are "grasped, never to be abandoned" by Amida. In other words, shinjin (the entrusting mind) is the mind that has attained the stage of non-retrogression. Shinran described it as "equal of perfect enlightenment."

It is wholehearted recitation so that our minds become whole and still with our mouths calling Buddha's name, eyes seeing Buddha's form, and ears hearing the nembutsu until the Pure Land appears. Since Amida Buddha and the Pure Land are always in our mind, Pure Land adherents describe

---

21. Hase and Conway, "Faith and Inochi as Infinite Life," 293.

this as "Amida in your own body." In this sense, wholehearted recitation is the very nembutsu chanting the nembutsu. Chanting the nembutsu is something in which we participate, not something that we produce. Amida is awakening to reality itself.

As I mentioned in chapter 3, this means that Amida Buddha is not a higher being as such. He is not felt as an ontological other or higher than the mind of the practitioner. The Buddhist doctrine of dependent origination (interrelated cause and effect) also applies to the Pure Land since Amida neither comes from any place nor goes anywhere else. Rather, he appears and disappears according to the existence or non-existence of causes, in this case, the presence of shinjin and a mind empty of self.

So ganying, the stimulus and response between things, ensures a sympathetic resonance from Amida. As you may have guessed by now, Japanese Buddhism borrowed ganying in the form of the Sino-Japanese loanword kanno. Hence, Zen masters such as Dogen who went to China employed this understanding in their teachings.

In fact, according to Professor Masanobu Takahashi, it is this compassionate and responsive nature of the dharmakaya that forms a commonality between Buddhist schools. He states that although zazen is assiduously practiced, the essential spirit of Zen is its belief in *jihi,* the mercy of the Buddha. In fact, this doctrine of jihi, he claims, is the point at which Zen, Pure Land, and Nichiren Buddhism converge.

In Japanese jihi means compassion and is a combination of two words. The first, *ji (maitri),* is the desire to bring about the well-being and happiness of others and *hi (karuna)* the desire to remove harm and suffering from others. Sometimes the word *daiji* or great mercy is also used which refers to a kind of mercy without distinction, thought to be available only to those having achieved buddhahood. The Amitayurdhyana Sutra (Sutra of Immeasurable Life as Told by the Buddha) teaches that Amida Buddha's mind is nothing but great jihi.

Pure Land Buddhists tend to phrase jihi in terms of mercy and benevolence whereas Zen practitioners in the West are more likely to avoid dualistic insinuations and perceive jihi as universal, unconditional compassion. Accordingly, jihi is also used in the expression *muen no jihi* which means compassion without emotional attachment, the non-preferential compassion exhibited by bodhisattvas and buddhas.

As Sheng-Yen pointed out, however, Buddha Name Recitation has a particular approach to the natural expression of compassion. It aims to invoke the compassionate presence of the buddha or bodhisattva to whom it is directed and is also capable of enlisting that buddha's power to help remove karmic obstacles and experience samadhi. In terms of bodhisattvas, for example, Kannon is considered the primary bodhisattva who cherishes the vow of universal jihi. It is believed by many Mahayana schools that Kannon is willing to answer all petitions and desires the salvation of every human being because she actualizes an ideal form of love.

In the case of sambhogakaya buddhas and bodhisattvas (such as Kannon), Zen Buddhism tends to perceive them in a metaphorical sense. That is, they are considered a metaphor or an archetype of an enlightened state in which a person abides in the knowledge that he/she is buddha nature itself. Consequently, in Zen, celestial buddhas and bodhisattvas are not so much transcendental beings as archetypes of certain aspects of buddha nature which are inherent in us, and which we can foster and develop. They are more reminders of our potential than divine beings.

Dogen strongly urged individuals to imbibe the spirit of Kannon in the daily actualization of the koan of life since the practice of wisdom (through the recognition of emptiness) is realized in the practice of jihi. In fact, he understood Kannon as more than just compassion but a symbol of a life force that is fundamental to living.

In the Himitsu Shobogenzo (28 Fascicle Secret Shobogenzo) however, Dogen lamented that in the house of the Buddha there is Bodhisattva Regarder of the Sounds of the World (Kannon). Few people have not seen her but very few people know her. Dogen knew that Kannon, the manifestation of compassion in the universe, is not external to us, she is us. So, it is not so much a case of faith *in* Kannon but faith *as* Kannon.

In the Saddharmapundarika Sutra (Lotus Sutra) used by Nichiren Buddhists, Kannon is described as a sambhogakaya figure who always comes to this world to save anyone who cries for help. In this sutra, Shakyamuni Buddha states that if any of the limitless hundreds of thousands of myriads of *koti* (ten million) of living beings who are undergoing all kinds of suffering hear of Kannon Bodhisattva and recite her name single-mindedly, she will immediately hear their voices and rescue them.

The sutra devotes an entire chapter to Kannon. It states that simply calling the name of the bodhisattva will be sufficient to save us from suffering and that Kannon takes on a great variety of forms to help us. The first is an expression of the compassion of Kannon, the second of her wisdom.

The sutra describes a total of thirty-three different manifestations to suit the minds of various beings and situations.

The late Nikkyo Niwano, the founder of Rissho Kosei-kai, a recent school of Nichiren adherents, taught that bodhisattvas are not gods from whom we should expect to receive special treatment, even in times of great trouble. Rather, they are models for how we ourselves can be bodhisattvas. Rather than praying to Kannon to save us from our own problems, the meaning of her thousand skills is that we should develop a thousand skills for helping others. In the very act of praying to Kannon to be relieved of suffering, there can be an element of wanting, like Kannon, to be compassionate toward others.

In this way, she is not only a symbol of compassion, but also compassion itself so that wherever compassion can be seen, Kannon can be seen. Interestingly, in the Vairocanabhisambodhi Sutra (Great Illuminator Sutra) Panduravasini (one of Kannon's forms known as White-robed Kannon) is the consort of Amida Buddha and is a symbol of the aspiration to enlightenment and the source of the buddhas and bodhisattvas.

Pure Land followers see Kannon as all merciful. She helps guide the person of faith on their road to the Pure Land of the Western Paradise. In this school of Buddhism, Kannon (representing compassion) forms part of a ruling triad along with Amida and the bodhisattva Mahasthamaprapta (representing wisdom), and images of the three are often placed together in temples. Thus, through prayer and devotion, Pure Land followers give birth to Amida, Kannon, and Mahasthamaprapta in their hearts, and foster the hope that the universe will respond with compassion.

In terms of vows, Zen, Nichiren, and Pure Land practice all involve compassionate vows in one form or another. In Zen, as I stated previously, practitioners take universal vows known as Shiguseiganmon, the Four Great Vows—to save all sentient beings, to end delusions, to master the teachings, and to abide by the Buddha Way.

Nichiren Buddhists also take the Shiguseiganmon, although according to Nichiren Daishonin, the practice of the bodhisattvas and the practice to accumulate good causes do not contain the four universal vows until the Saddharmapundarika Sutra (Lotus Sutra) is fully embraced. In Pure Land Buddhism, followers make the Pure Land Four Great Vows—to be reborn into the Pure Land, to save all sentient beings, to see Amida Buddha at the moment of death, and to abide by the Buddha Way.

In the previous chapter, I mentioned that buddhas and bodhisattvas also take vows to lead living beings to enlightenment and that there are two kinds of vows: universal and individual. Among individual vows, the forty-eight vows of Amida Buddha (to deliver to the Pure Land all who call on his name) and the twelve vows of Medicine Master Buddha in the Saddharmapundarika Sutra (Lotus Sutra) (to heal the sicknesses of humankind) are well known. Such vows made by buddhas while engaged in bodhisattva practice in previous lives are called original vows.

All compassionate vows, whether original or universal, are based on the equality of liberation. In Zen, the recognition of the buddha nature of every person is considered to lead to the knowledge of the basic equality of all people. Nichiren believed that the Saddharmapundarika Sutra (Lotus Sutra) contained the essence of all of Shakyamuni's teachings related to the laws of causality and karma, without any distinction to enlightenment. The sutra states that just as rain falls on all vegetation, so the Eternal or Cosmic Buddha's compassion extends equally to all people.

This universal potential is a part of Pure Land doctrine too in terms of an equal capacity to be saved by Amida. The Amitayurdhyana Sutra (Sutra of Immeasurable Life as Told by the Buddha) points out that since the mind of Amida Buddha with all its boundless potentialities of love and wisdom is compassion itself, Buddha can save all. Consider the following quote from Honen Shonin.

> There shall be no distinction, no regard to male or female, good
> or bad, exalted or lowly; none shall fail to be in his Land of Purity
> after having called, with complete faith, on Amida Buddha.[22]

Shandao, the de-facto founder of the Pure Land school, wrote in his Wu-bu Jiu-juan (Five Works in Nine Fascicles) that whether human or celestial, wholesome or unwholesome, all will be reborn and that in the Pure Land, no differences separate them. All of us walk on the irreversible path to buddhahood because this Earth is the Pure Land and we ourselves are buddhahood.

Compare this with Bodhidharma's Wuxing Lun (Treatise on Awakening to the Nature of Mind) which points out that while the world sees that there's male and female, rich and poor, the Way does not. It makes no distinction and because of this, everyone is capable of realization. In all three traditions faith is liberation and equality.

22. Okazaki, *Pure Land Buddhist Painting,* 14.

As an essential aspect of both reality and practice, Zen practitioners have faith that buddha nature, the quality of universal emptiness, guarantees all can equally be liberated once they raise the aspiration for awakening, that is, bodaishin, the great faith mind. From different angles and through different methods, the quality of equivalency in terms of liberational potential is present.

For Nichiren Buddhists, this liberation relies on three fundamentals—faith, practice, and study. The Saddharmapandarika Sutra (Lotus Sutra) tells us that whoever has faith in the sutra will achieve buddhahood. Nichiren considered faith the most fundamental attribute for the attainment of buddhahood and, like many in Zen, recognized the inseparability and mutually supportive roles of faith and practice. Faith gives rise to practice and study, he pointed out, and practice and study serve to deepen faith.

In the sutra Shakyamuni addresses Shariputra, an arhat who was known as foremost in wisdom: "Even you, Shariputra, in the case of this sutra were able to gain entrance through faith alone. How much more so, then, the other voice-hearers." In other words, if someone such as Shariputra who does not know the Mahayana Way and is seemingly conceptually constrained by his previous religious training, can reach enlightenment through faith in the sutra, so can anyone. The Cosmic Buddha acts on our behalf if we have faith that that is what will happen.

To Nichiren Buddhists, to understand reality by faith for even a moment i.e., to have a single moment of faith and joy in the message of the Saddharmapundarika Sutra (Lotus Sutra) is a practice superior to other practices typically associated with Buddhism. The chapter *Distinctions in Benefits* states that "if there are living beings who, on hearing that the life span of the Buddha is of such long duration, are able to believe and understand it even for a moment, the benefits they gain thereby will be without limit or measure."

In fact, in the sutra, Shakyamuni Buddha states that anyone who understands by faith for even a moment of thought will obtain more merits than those who practice the first five of the six perfections and will never falter in walking the way to unsurpassed perfect awakening.

As mentioned previously, Zen uses the term *ichinenshin* to describe an instant consciousness of faith that necessarily results in perfect buddhahood. In Nichiren Buddhism, the term *ichinensanzen* describes a similar principle. Ichinensanzen is the theoretical formulation of the key insight of the Saddharmapundarika Sutra (Lotus Sutra), that is, the practice of introspection into the essence of mind.

First described by the renowned sixth-century Buddhist scholar Zhiyi, ichinen sanzen or the three thousand modes of existence in a single moment demonstrates that the entire phenomenal world exists in a single moment of life. *Ichi* means one and signifies the one ultimate truth or the middle way of the Dharma nature. This doctrine teaches that all life is endowed with all phenomena of reality i.e., the three thousand different realms.

Thus, the realization of inchinensanzen is the realization of interdependent reality—that body and mind, cause and effect, subject and object, sentient and non-sentient are mutually encompassed in every moment of thought. When we investigate the interconnected nature of the universe, we see that even within us are a multitude of universes, each producing and manifesting in its own way. In this way, we come to recognize not only our buddha nature but the realization of the buddha-land in this world. After all, the sutra tells us, the sole cause for buddhas entering the world of suffering is to enable us to fully realize buddha nature.

Moreover, whenever someone shows sincere faith in the Buddha by performing a good deed, no matter how small (bowing, even coloring an image of the Buddha) this act also sets them on the path to Buddhahood. In fact, there is no time that the Eternal Buddha does not react to faith.

Unsurprisingly, faith, vows, and practice form the cornerstone of Pure Land as well. If these three conditions are fulfilled, rebirth in the land of ultimate bliss will be achieved. In terms of faith and vow, as we now know, Pure Land followers have faith that all can be free from suffering through the compassion of Amida Buddha if their practice is to truly embody shinjin or the trusting mind. Master Zhixu explained the relationship between faith and vows.

> Without faith, we are not sufficiently equipped to take vows. With
> out vows, we are not sufficiently equipped to guide our practice.
> Without the wondrous practice of reciting the Buddha-name, we
> are not sufficiently equipped to fulfill our vows and bring our faith
> to fruition.[23]

Thus, great faith is one with great practice. While Zen points to a relationship between the level of faith, doubt and determination and the level of

---

23. Zhixu, *Mind Seal of the Buddha*, 16.

realization, it is thought by some Pure Land adherents that achieving rebirth in the Pure Land depends on faith and vows, while the level of rebirth (in terms of ease of conditions in the Pure Land) depends on the depth of practice.

Naturally, merit and virtue are also a part of Pure Land doctrine. Rennyo Shonin, a descendant of Shinran Shonin and the eighth Head Priest of the Honganji Pure Land Temple, pointed out that *hotsuganeko*, turning merit towards Amida, entails the transference of virtues and merit from Amida Buddha at the moment of total reliance. In other words, we acquire the Tathagata's virtues through entrusting ourselves to his vow-power.

The Kuan Hsin Funshu (Commentary to the Treatise on Discerning the Mind) suggests that when the practitioner takes up mindfulness of a particular buddha through chanting a buddha's name, they must grasp the fact that the merits of this buddha are fully equivalent to the merits of all the buddhas of the ten directions. In other words, if buddha recitation is one-pointed, the paramitas are fully present.

For example, it is said that by completely focusing on chanting the nembutsu or visualizing Amida Buddha, we fulfil the paramita of discipline (*sila*), and cannot commit negative karmic acts or violate the precepts. Likewise, reciting Amida's name wholeheartedly allows us to fulfil the paramita of concentration (*dyana*) since we have a completely focused mind. Accordingly, when a practitioner's mind becomes still it leads to the perfection or paramita of wisdom (prajna).

Nembutsu practice, therefore, is both a means to an end as well as the end itself manifested in daily life. In the Kyogoshinsho (The Collection of Passages Expounding the True Teaching, Living, Faith, and Realization of the Pure Land), Shinran teaches that great practice is the nembutsu because it is the product of the supreme enlightenment of Amida Buddha. Since this practice is the "treasure ocean of virtues of the reality of suchness," these are instantly matured when the nembutsu is said. Practice is inseparable from faith, and cause and effect are one. Academic Paul Groner termed this the shortening of the path, that is, the equating of the beginning of the path with the end.

Since the beginning and the end are the same, it is essential of course, to raise the mind of faith, the bodhi mind. Having learned what bodaishin and doshin in Zen mean, what do a Pure Land and a Nichiren practitioner mean by them and how are they related to faith?

In the case of Nichiren Buddhism, Nichiren advised that if we wish to free ourselves from the sufferings of birth and death and to attain enlightenment, we must perceive the truth that is originally inherent in all living beings. This truth is namu myoho renge kyo. Chanting namu myoho renge kyo enables us to grasp the truth innate in all life. To chant with total faith is raising the mind of enlightenment which in turn is the mind of great faith that recognizes the universal law of the Saddhamapundarika Sutra (Lotus Sutra).

This title namu myoho renge kyo is considered the heart of the sutra and the seed of Buddhahood and contains all the practices the Buddha undertook in the stages of cultivation as well as the merits he achieved. The implication, therefore, is that a person who embraces the *daimoku* (namu myoho renge kyo) of the sutra necessarily receives the merits of the Buddha and realizes Buddhahood.

Nichiren taught that the Lotus Sutra exists in every one of us and that when we realize this truth we come into the presence of the Eternal Buddha. In fact, the *Ten Merits* chapter of the Lotus Sutra states that the sutra can make a person give rise to the mind of the ten virtues of compassion, non-attachment and wisdom, of liberating others, as well as the mind of diligence.

So, while the sutra speaks of recognizing one's own nature, it is interesting to note that faith and the chanting of the daimoku do not take as their object the practitioner's own mind as in Zen meditation, but the heart of the sutra, the Eternal Buddha revealed in last fourteen chapters of the sutra. These two, dharma and buddha, may be understood as two aspects of the same truth.

In Pure Land Buddhism, awakening the bodhi mind is seen in terms of awakening the aspiration for birth (*yokusho*) in the Pure Land. Shinran taught that deeply entrusting oneself to Amida's compassionate vow and aspiring to become a buddha is called aspiration for enlightenment.

According to Shinran, since shinjin is the mind that aspires to attain Buddhahood, it is in turn the mind aspiring for great enlightenment of what he called a "crosswise leap of faith," the cutting through to reality with faith in a manner somewhat reminiscent of the sudden enlightenment of patriarchal Zen.

Accordingly, Pure Land Master Yinguang reminded his students not to be surprised that a single recitation of the nembutsu surpasses the ten stages of faith on the path of the bodhisattvas since the nembutsu's six letters (in Chinese) encompass the three vehicles of the sravaka, pratyekabuddha, and bodhisattva. This is how a person gains a sense of their own buddha nature, which is also the buddha-mind given to the practitioner.

Moreover, since shinjin is equivalent to the mind that aspires for Buddhahood, it is, at the same time, bodhicitta, the mind to save sentient beings. Since the mind of Amida is compassion, it stands to reason that for ganying or correlative resonance to be a reality, the adherent's mind must also be compassionate. The Tannisho (Lamentations of Divergences), an important Pure Land text, states the following about the Pure Land of mind and its relation to bodaishin and jihi.

> We are enlightened the moment we become one with the all-illuminating, all-pervading light of the bright moon of truth shining forth as the dark clouds of tormenting cravings are dispersed when we reach the shore of the Pure Land of Fulfilment. For having crossed over the turbulent sea of suffering that is life-and-death on the vessel of Amida's Grand Compassion, we are enabled to save every sentient being.[24]

It is bodaishin, the bodhi mind of faith, which seeks to save all sentient beings and bring them to birth in the Pure Land. Thus, to attain buddhahood in Pure Land Buddhism also means to bring others to the attainment of buddhahood. Chanting the nembutsu is the path for the perfect fulfillment of practices of self-benefit and the benefiting-of-others.

This is also where self-power (*joriki* or *jiriki*) and other-power (*tariki*) come into play. Historically, schools of Buddhism have been divided into those who rely on self-power and those who rely on other-power—the assistance of buddhas and bodhisattvas. Most Buddhist schools tend to be placed in the first category while faith-based schools place themselves in the second.

Zen, for example, is usually placed in the self-power group since progress along the path of enlightenment is achieved through intense and sustained personal effort by actualizing buddha nature in every moment. Despite the common perception of complete reliance on other-power, however, esoteric and Pure Land schools combine self-effort with other-power.

Notice that I used the term self-effort rather than self-power. Reverend Joren MacDonald of the Florin Buddhist Temple makes a useful distinction between them. Self-power is the energy and discipline utilized to reach enlightenment by our own power in this current life. Self-effort,

24. Williams, *Mahayana Buddhism: The Doctrinal Foundations*, 274.

however, is what we must utilize to function at a human level. We need our will and conscious reasoning to operate in the activities of our daily life, although they are not enough in themselves for realization.

By combining self-effort with other-power, buddhahood can be realized because other-power is the immeasurable indescribable infinite wisdom and compassion always surrounding us and embracing us. The Avatamsaka Sutra (Flower Garland Sutra) points out that the mind of faith is the mind of sincerity; it is a deep mind, a mind that is sincerely glad to be led to Buddha's Pure Land by his power. Faith is thus only real when the otherness or transcendence of other-power is preserved.

This is why even a moment of faith will lead us to the Western Paradise because, in that one moment of unity, the self is forgotten. Dogen noted in his Genjokoan (Actualizing the Fundamental Point) that there can be no more powerful form of self-forgetting than abandoning oneself completely to the Other.

It is worth noting, however, that despite all the rhetoric, the line between self-effort, self-power, and other-power is not entirely definitive. While Zen is usually perceived as a self-power practice, blurred boundaries between self and other practices exist. The late Sheng-Yen in a chapter entitled *Faith and Chan* wrote that many people think Zen practice depends only on their own efforts, requiring self-reliance while those who recite the nembutsu depend solely on external help. Both are incorrect. Zen practice requires external help while nembutsu practice requires one's own effort.

According to Sheng-Yen, a person can hardly become an accomplished practitioner purely through just their own effort since efficacious practice makes use of a teacher and a sangha. In fact, he asserts, practicing Zen by depending solely on one's own efforts without believing in the power of the buddhas and bodhisattvas cannot be considered practicing Buddhism at all.[25]

In a chapter entitled *Self power and Other Power*, the late Albert Low, Zen Master and director at the Montreal Zen Center, described his awakening to the presence of other-power in Zen practice. He perfectly describes a modern Zen-in-the-West awakening to Mahayana faith:

> I well remember, in the early days of practice, sitting with the feeling of having been conned into something, conned into practicing Zen. I had this feeling because, when I first started practicing seriously, I was somewhat imbued with D. T. Suzuki's idea of

25. Sheng-Yen, *Chan Practice and Faith*, 4.

'self-power' as opposed to 'other power' as the true spiritual way. Self-power seemed, at the time, to be highly desirable, because it promised to do away with all need for faith and belief. I was on my own and I could rely on myself alone.

Then, much to my dismay, after I had started the practice, the teacher began to talk to me about faith. I could not help wondering what faith had to do with self-power . . . More and more it seemed that he was telling me that my so-called self-power was somehow the problem, and that I had to surrender it or let it go. Gradually, over the years, it began to dawn on me that faith and belief are quite different and that what had been called self-power was really other-power because I realized that what was referred to as 'Buddha nature' was beyond, or transcended 'me' as I knew myself to be on a day-to-day basis.[26]

This is supported by Francis Dojun Cook who maintains that Dogen spent his life teaching a Buddhism of faith in the power of the other. Faith is important in Dogen's Zen, he tells us, because practice must be undertaken in trust in another—the Buddha. This is the necessary basis of practice. Seen in this way, Cook maintains that Dogen's Zen is not really the Buddhism of self-power; it is the Buddhism of other-power. "One may indeed practice the Buddhism of self-power, and many do, but it will not be Dogen's way."[27]

As Dogen stated, we must know that the roots of faith do not grow in oneself or in others or through our own efforts. Enlightenment is already intrinsic. What matters is that we become aware of it. For Dogen, we can only talk about right faith when the entire body becomes faith. Where faith appears, so do the buddhas and ancestors. Or, as Pure Land practitioners might say, between birth in the Pure Land of an ordinary person and of a great master, there is no difference if they have shinjin.

So, although Dogen advocated zazen, that did not mean he was solely advocating a self-power practice through which practitioners accomplish realization purely through their own efforts. Rather, he also stressed the devoted acceptance of and support from three main other sources: the lineage of historical buddhas and ancestors, the cosmic buddhas and bodhisattvas, and, as I will explain in the next paragraph, the phenomenal world of the environment informed by buddha-dharma.

26. Low, *Beyond The God Delusion*, 26.

27. Cook, *How to Raise an Ox*, 24.

All three traditions make use of what is known as a buddha field, which in East Asian Buddhism came to be known as a Pure Land. Ideas and practices related to purified buddha-realms exist in every form of Mahayana Buddhism. A pure land is also called a field of good fortune which is a simile for that which enables people to gain good fortune. This field contains the blessings that arise from good actions. A buddha, for example, is often referred to as a great field of good fortune, as well as any Buddhist practice that gives rise to positive outcomes. So, expressing wisdom through good deeds, conduct, service, and teaching to others, makes them our field of merit.

This concept is not new. In early Buddhist texts, there are numerous references to the buddhas of the ten directions. The notion of a single universe with long intervals between the appearance of buddhas necessarily entailed that there were buddhas living and teaching the Dharma in other worlds. Consequently, the concept of multitudes of celestial buddhas and their buddha-fields throughout the cosmos can be found in the earliest Mahayana texts.

This inclusion of buddha fields in Mahayana sutras also meant that Buddha came to be considered as one incarnation of a transcendent cosmic buddha field, buddha nature, which is always working and in all worlds for the liberation of everyone. Thus, on an essential level, ultimately all fields are one field, and one field is all fields.

The sutras of Pure Land teach that, as the celestial example of buddhahood in the Western Paradise, Amida expounds the Dharma in his buddha-field or pure land. The Longer Sukhavativyuha Sutra describes this as a land of beauty that surpasses all other realms. It is said to be inhabited by many gods, people, flowers, and fruits. The Shorter Sukhavativyuha Sutra points out that the Pure Land is full of trees and that even the birds and fish speak words of the Dharma.

This is an ideal environment in which to practice Buddhism. Each element of this environment can be regarded as a metaphor for an aspect of the Buddhist Path. The Western Paradise means the moral nature, confirmed, pure and at rest. Amida Buddha is the mind, clear and enlightened while the rows of trees stand for the mind cultivating virtues. Music in the Pure Land can be considered the harmony of virtues in the mind while the flowers, particularly the lotus, represent the mind opening to consciousness and intelligence. The beautiful birds mean the mind becoming changed and renewed.

The concept of a buddha field also exists in Nichiren Buddhism as well, albeit in a different way. The Saddamapundarika Sutra (Lotus Sutra) states that all things confirm and reveal the one vehicle of enlightenment i.e., they lead to Buddhahood. This means that everything is a teisho of the Cosmic Buddha. An old Zen saying tells us that the Buddha's preaching is the murmuring of the stream and the color of the mountain.

As Taigen Dan Leighton, author and scholar, points out, the inconceivable lifespan of the Cosmic Buddha in this sutra supports a view of a present place and time that can function as a non-dual and integrated realm of realization—a variety of pure land. This realm is realized through faith in namu myoho renge kyo, the cosmic law of the Saddamapundarika Sutra (Lotus Sutra).

In chapter 16 of the sutra, the Buddha states that when beings desire with a unified or undivided mind to see and meet the Buddha, at that time he appears with the great assembly at Vulture Peak and expounds the sutra. Dogen considered this undivided mind as Vulture Peak itself.

Thus, when Nichiren Buddhists totally embody faith, they recognize that the sutra is not separate from the world and neither does it describe a transcendent realm outside of itself. It is itself the embodiment of the awakening aspect of the phenomenal i.e., the text represents and enacts the world's liberational potential. So just the text itself is considered a field of good fortune. Holding, using, and reciting the text is reciting the entire universe.

Dogen took an interesting Zen tack on buddha fields. Dogen taught that space is form itself, concretely physical, and not separate from the dynamic effort of aspiration and practice. So, what we do in that space has an effect. Some Zen practitioners speak of feeling a presence in the *zendo* after a long period of sitting, for example. For Dogen, this reflects the fact that when beings awaken to buddhahood, their realization affects the environment around them i.e., it becomes a field of good fortune.

This means that zazen influences not only the people around the practitioner, but also, insentient things such as grass, trees, fences and walls, tiles, and pebbles. In turn, the space that we practice in is alive and supportive of dharma practice. We can see why Dogen utilized the notion of kanno doko since the meditator and the elements of the world intimately and imperceptibly assist each other.

For Dogen, the whole universe in the ten directions is filled with the limitlessly abundant eyes of Kannon and is itself an organ of compassion which responds to Zen practice. This also means that taking care of the phenomenal world is the natural expression of the practice of zazen. Faith is a kind of active practice relationship with space so that a practitioner receives support when acting from that space of faith.

Extrapolating from this, Dogen considered sutras or scriptures as not just written materials but all manifestations of the universe itself. Scriptures are the sources from which we may learn the message of the Buddha and attain enlightenment. Sutras are none other than the body of the Tathagata, and through our encounter with them, we encounter the Buddha. The whole universe is a responsive buddha-field.

10

Faithful Conclusion

CONSIDERING THE FAITH, VOW, and practice of all three traditions, we can see that Zen, Pure Land and Nichiren Buddhisms are themselves the many fields of good fortune. As a Zen practitioner, I am reassured to know that when a person recites the name of Buddha with wisdom and faith, they can be in the presence of Buddha. I also recognize the deep lessons of the lotus—that there are three thousand worlds in a single moment and that all vehicles are the one vehicle of awakening.

In terms of which practice is best, however, I think it prudent to leave you with some words from Zen Master Dainin Katagiri:

> A student challenged Katagiri Roshi saying, "We are often duped by devotion." Katagiri Roshi responded, "You are too much involved in your individual world. Very much. Too much. Your understanding is not wide-ranging. Not only you, if a person's understanding is very narrow, you are duped by whatever it is— Dharma, Christianity, or even the self."[1]

Considering that Soto founder Keizan gave Soto Zen an appeal based on faith and devotion (he openly described his devout faith in Kannon) as well as meditation, Katagiri is reminding us that our preconceived notions of something, in this case, faith-based practice, can dupe us into seeing only what we want to see.

In the Itivuttaka (The Short Discourses) of the Pali Canon, the Buddha gave this advice:

1. Port, *Keep Me in Your Heart A While*, 87.

> If you seek after truth, you should investigate things in such a
> way that your consciousness as you investigate is not distracted
> by what you find or diffused and scattered; neither is it fixed and
> set. For the one who is not swayed, there will be a transcending of
> birth, death, and time.[2]

Perhaps, then, if we are going to judge the faith of Zen, it should be done
not by what we think Zen faith is, but in accordance with the basic, bottom
line of Buddhism—its effectiveness as a means of eliminating greed, hatred,
and delusion in favor of ceasing to do evil and learning to do good. It is my
hope that this book contributes to that evaluation.

2. Bancroft, *The Buddha Speaks: A Book of Guidance*, 118.

Some Texts That Mention Faith

Abhidharmakosa-bhasya (Verses on the Treasury of Abhidharma)

Abhisamaya-alamkara (Ornament of Realization)

Amitayurdhyana Sutra (The Sutra of Visualizing the Buddha of Infinite Life and Light)

Anunatva Apurnatva Nirdesa (Sutra of Non-Decrease, Non-Increase)

Astadasasahasrika Prajnaparamita Sutra (The 18,000-Line Prajnaparamita Sutra)

Avatamsaka Sutra (Flower Garland Sutra)

Bendowa (Discourse on the Practice of the Way)

Brahmajala Sutra (Brahma Net Sutra)

Chanshi Chanyao (Three Essentials of Chan)

Chanzha Shane Yebao Jing (Sutra of Detecting Good or Evil Karma and Requital)

Cheng Weishi Lun (Discourse on the Perfection of Consciousness-only)

Chewu Chanshi Yulu (The Recorded Sayings of Chan Master Jixing Chewu)

Chuanxinfayao (Treatise on the Essentials of the Transmission of Mind)

Dasheng Qixin Lun (The Awakening of Mahayana Faith)

Erru Sixing Lun (Treatise on the Two Entrances and Four Practices)

Gakudo Yojinshu (Points to Watch in Practicing the Way)

Genjokoan (Actualizing the Fundamental Point)

Gisillon So (A Commentary on the Awakening of Faith in the Mahayana)

Jin'ganbei (Diamond Scalpel Treatise)

Kyogoshinsho (The Collection of Passages Expounding the True Teaching, Living, Faith, and Realization of the Pure Land)

Kuan Hsin Lun (Sutra of Contemplation of Mind)

Lalitavistara (Extensive Play)

Lankavatara Sutra (The Sutra of the Descent to Lanka)

Lengjia Shiziji (Record of Master and Disciple in the Transmission of the Lanka)

Longshu Zengguang Jingtu Wen (Awakening of Faith in the Pure Land)

Mahayana Samparigraha Shastra (Commentary on the Compendium of the Great Vehicle)

Mahayana Satadharma Prakasamukha Shastra (Lucid Introduction to the One Hundred Dharmas)

Mahaparinibbana Sutra ((Buddha's Last Days)

Mahaparinirvana Sutra (Sutra of the Great Decease)

Mahaprajnaparamita Shastra (Treatise on the Perfection of Great Wisdom)

Mahaprajnaparamita Sutra (Heart of Great Wisdom Sutra)

Maharatnakuta Sutra (Sutra of Assembled Treasures)

Mohe Zhiguan (Great Calming and Contemplation)

Muryangsu Gyeong Jongyo (Doctrinal Essentials of the Sutra of Immeasurable Life)

Pratyutpanna Samadhi Sutra (Sutra of the Samadhi of Being in the Presence of All Buddhas)

Pusa Yingluo Benye Jing (Bodhisattvas' Diadem Primary Activities Sutra)

Ratnagotravibhaga (Manual of the Ultimate Doctrine)

Ratnavali (Precious Garland)

Ratnolka-dharani (The Formulae of the Three Jewels)

Renwang Jing (Prajnaparamita Sutra on How Benevolent Kings May Protect Their Countries)

Saddharmapundarika Sutra (Lotus Sutra)

Samdhinirmocana Sutra (Sutra of the Explanation of the Profound Secrets)

Satapancasatka (Matrceta's Hymn to the Buddha)

Shobogenzo (Treasure of the True Dharma Eye)

Shumon Mujintoron (The Inexhaustible Lamp of Zen)

Sikshasamuccaya (Compendium of Precepts)

Srimaladevi Sutra (The Lion's Roar of Queen Srimala)

Son'ga Kwigam (The Mirror of Zen)

Sukhavativyuha Sutra (Longer Infinite Life Sutra)

Sukhavativyuha Sutra (Shorter Amitabha Sutra)

Surangama Samadhi Sutra (Samadhi of the Heroic Progression)

Tannisho (Lamentations of Divergences)

Trimsika-karika (Thirty Verses)

Vajracchedika Prajnaparamita Sutra (Diamond Sutra)

Vijnaptimatratasiddhi Shastra (Treatise on the Establishment of the Doctrine of Mere Consciousness)

Wuxing Lun (Treatise on Awakening to the Nature of Mind)

Xinxin Ming (Verses on the Faith in Mind)

Zhengdaoge (Song of Enlightenment)

Zhiguan Fuxing Zhuan Hongjue (Commentary on the Great Calming and Contemplation)

Zongjng Lu (Records of the Source-Mirror)

Bibliography

Asociación Zen Taisen Deshimaru. "Kesa: The Monk's Robe." Accessed October 23, 2019. https://zenkan.com/en/zazen-en/kesa/.

Aturupana, Senevi. "Saddha: An Analytical Study of Its Role in Theravada Buddhism." PhD diss., University of London, 2005.

Bancroft, Anne, ed. *The Buddha Speaks: A Book of Guidance from the Buddhist Scriptures.* Boston: Shambhala, 2000.

Baroni, Helen Josephine. *Obaku Zen: The Emergence of the Third Sect of Zen in Tokugawa, Japan.* Hawaii: University of Hawai'i Press, 2000.

Baskind, James. "The Nianfo in Obaku Zen: A Look at the Teachings of the Three Founding Masters." *Japanese Religions* 33, no. 1 & 2 (2008) 19–34.

Bender, Courtney and Wendy Cadge. "Constructing Buddhism(s): Interreligious Dialogue and Religious Hybridity." *Sociology of Religion* 67, no. 3 (2006), 229–247.

Bloom, Alfred. "Faith: It's Arising." In *Vol. 1, Critical Readings on Pure Land Buddhism in Japan*, edited by Galen Amstutz. The Netherlands: Brill, 2020.

Bercholz, Samuel and Sherab Chodzin Kohn, eds. *An Introduction to the Buddha and His Teachings.* USA: Barnes & Noble, 1993.

Blyth, Reginal Horace. *Vol. 5, Zen and Zen Classics.* Tokyo: Hokuseido Press, 1960.

Borup, Jorn. *Japanese Rinzai Zen Buddhism: Myoshinji, A Living Religion.* Boston: Leiden, 2008.

Bukkyo Dendo Kyokai, *The Teaching of Buddha.* 351st rev. ed. Tokyo: Bukkyo Dendo Kyokai, 1966.

Carlson, Kyogen. *Zen in the American Grain: Discovering the Teachings at Home.* New York: Station Hill Press, 1994.

Carpenter, Amber D. "Faith Without God in Nagarjuna." In *Thomism and Asian Cultures*, edited by Alfredo Co and Paolo Bolano. Manila: University of Santo Tomas, 2012.

Cleary, Thomas. *Entry into the Inconceivable: An Introduction to Hua-yen Buddhism.* Honolulu: University of Hawaii Press, 1983.

———. *Kensho: The Heart of Zen.* Boston: Shambhala, 1977.

Cohen, Jundo. "What's Often Missing in Shikantaza Explanations." Accessed 12 December, 2020. https://www.treeleaf.org/forums/showthread.php?15111-WHAT-s-OFTEN-MISSING-in-SHIKANTAZA-EXPLANATIONS.

Conze, Edward, ed. *Buddhist Texts Through the Ages.* Translated by Edward Conze. New York: Harper and Row, 1964.

Cook, Francis Dojun. *How to Raise an Ox: Zen Practice as Taught in Master Dogen's Shobogenzo.* Chicago: Wisdom Publications, 1999.

BIBLIOGRAPHY

Cooper, Andrew. "Understanding Nichiren Buddhism." *Tricycle: The Buddhist Review*. Accessed June 13, 2019. https://tricycle.org/trikedaily/understanding-nichiren-buddhism.

Cutts, Eijun Linda. "Sewing Buddha's Robe." Accessed January 10, 2018. https://austinzencenter.org/sewing-buddhas-robe/.

Dogen, Kigen. *Shobogenzo: The Treasure House of the Eye of the True Teaching*. Translated by Hubert Nearman. USA: Shasta Abbey, 2007.

Faure, Bernard. *The Rhetoric of Immediacy: A Cultural Critique of Chan/Zen Buddhism*. Princeton: Princeton University Press, 1991.

Foulk, T. Griffith. "Ritual in Japanese Zen Buddhism." In *Zen Ritual: Studies of Zen Buddhist Theory in Practice*, edited by Steven Heine and Dale S. Wright. Oxford: Oxford University Press, 2008.

Furuta, Shokin. *Zen to Jōdo* 禅と浄土 [Zen and the Pure Land]. Tōkyō: Shunjūsha, 1960.

Giustarinin, Giuliano. "Faith and Renunciation in Early Buddhism: Saddha and Nekkhamma." *Rivista di Studi Sudasiatici* 1, (2006) 161–179.

Gomez, Luis. "Faith." In *Encyclopedia of Buddhism*, edited by Robert E. Buswell, 277–279. New York: Macmillan Reference USA, 2004.

Grumbach, Lisa. "Nenbutsu and Meditation: Problems with the Categories of Contemplation, Devotion, Meditation and Faith." *Pacific World: Third Series* 7, (2005) 91–105.

Hangthukmod, Phramaha Thawatchai. *The Importance of Saddha in Theravada Buddhism: An Analytical Study*. Calcutta: University of Calcutta, 2015.

Hartman, Zenkei Blanche. "Foreword." Accessed January 10, 2018. http://www.buddhasrobeissewn.org/html/about.html.

Hase, Shoto and Conway, Michael. "Faith and Inochi as Infinite Life." *The Eastern Buddhist* 45, no. 1 (2014) 275–298.

Heng-ching, Shih. "Yung-ming's Syncretism of Pure Land and Ch'an." *The Journal of the International Association of Buddhist Studies* 10, no. 1 (1987) 117–134.

Hirakawa, Akira. *A History of Indian Buddhism from Sakyamuni to Early Mahayana*. Translated by Paul Groner. Hawaii: University of Hawaii Press, 1990.

Ingram, Paul. "The Zen Critique of Pure Land Buddhism." *Journal of the American Academy of Religion* 41, (1973) 184–200.

Jorgenson, John, ed. *Hyujeong: Selected Works*. Translated by John Jorgensen. Korea: Jogye Order of Korean Buddhism, 2012.

Joskovitch, Erez Hekigan. "The Inexhaustible Lamp of Faith: Faith and Awakening in the Japanese Rinzai Tradition." *Japanese Journal of Religious Studies* 32, (2015) 319–338.

Kang, Munsun. "On the Meaning of "Faith" in Early Ch'an." *International Journal of Buddhist Thought and Culture* 12, (2009) 95–109.

Kapleau, Philip. *The Three Pillars of Zen*. Boston: Beacon, 1965.

Karunaratna, Indumathie. "Devotion." In *Vol. IV, Encyclopaedia of Buddhism*, edited by Gunapala Piyasena Malalaskera, 435–437. Sri Lanka: Government of Ceylon, 1979.

Katagiri, Dainin. *Returning To Silence: Zen Practice in Daily Life*. Boston: Shambhala, 1989.

Katagiri, Tomoe. *Study of the Okesda: Nyohoe-The Buddha's Robe*. USA: Minnesota Zen Center, 2015.

Kim, Hee-jin. *Eihei Dogen: Mystical Realist*. Boston: Wisdom, 2004.

Kim, Young-suk. "Wonhyo's Human Character Education: Principles and Practice Methods." *International Journal of Buddhist Thought & Culture* 4, (2004) 141–163.

Kimura, Kiyotaka. "Faith and Enlightenment in Dogen's Shobogenzo." In *Faith in Buddhism,* edited by Imre Hamar and Takami Inoue, 153–164. Budapest: Institute for East Asian Studies, 2016.

Kinst, Daijaku. *Trust, Realization and the Self in Soto Zen Practice.* USA: Institute of Buddhist Studies, 2015.

Koh, Seunghak. *Li Tongxuan's (635–730) Thought and His Place in the Huayan Tradition of Chinese Buddhism.* PhD diss., University of California, Los Angeles, 2011.

Koho, Keido Chisan. *Soto Zen: An Introduction to the Thought of the Serene Reflection Meditation School of Buddhism,* edited by Jisho Perry. Mount Shasta: Shasta Abbey, 2000.

Kuang, Yin. *Pure-Land Zen, Zen Pure-Land: Letters from Patriarch Yin Kuang.* Translated by Van Hien Study Group. New York: Van Hien Study Group, 1993.

Kubovcakova, Zuzana. "Believe It or Not: Dogen on the Question of Faith." *Studia Orientalia Slovaca* 17, no. 2 (2018) 193–215.

Largen, Kristin Johnston. "Appreciation and Appropriation: Christian "Borrowing" of Buddhist Practices." *Pacific World Third Series* 15, (2013), 105–116.

Leighton, Taigen Dan. *Visions of Awakening Space and Time: Dogen and the Lotus Sutra.* London: Oxford University Press, 2008.

Low, Albert. *Beyond The God Delusion: Religion as the Quest for Transcendence.* USA: Smashwords, 2009.

MacPhillamy, Daizui. "Tunnel Vision: The Surprise of Devotion in Zen." *Ascent Magazine* (2007). https://ascentmagazine.com/articles.aspx%3FarticleID=90&page=read&sub page=past&issueID=10.html.

Masutani, Fumio. *A Comparative Study of Buddhism and Christianity.* Tokyo: Young East Assoc., 1957.

Mizuno, Kogen. *Essentials of Buddhism.* Tokyo: Kosei, 1996.

Muller, Charles A. "Right View (samyak-drsti) and Correct Faith (sraddha): Correspondence, Distinction, and Re-Merging in East Asian Mahayana." Accessed September 2, 2016. http://www.acmuller.net/articles/2015–11-06-toho-gakkai-faith-as-a-kind-of-view—presentation.html.

Naong, Hyegeun. "A Letter to Minister Mok In-gil." Translated by Jogye Order of Korean Buddhism. Accessed June 26, 2023. http://www.koreanbuddhism.net/bbs/board,php?bo_table=0020&wr_id=4&sst=wr_datetime&sod=desc&sop=and&pa ge=7.

Ng, Edwin. "Buddhism, Poststructuralist Thought, Cultural Studies: A Profession of Faith." *Cultural Studies Review* 18, no. 2 (2012) 109–128.

Nishitani, Keiji. *Vol. 11, Nishitani Keiji Chosakushū.* 西谷啓治著作集 [Collected Works of Nishitani Keiji]. Tōkyō: Sōbunsha, 1987.

Nordberg, Mauno. "Is Dhamma a Religion?" *Light of the Dhamma* 1, no. 3 (1953), 40–41.

Nye, Malory. *Religion: The Basics.* Oxford: Routledge, 2004.

Oda, Akihiro. "The Concept of "Faith" in the Discourse on the Awakening of Mahayana Faith." In *Faith in Buddhism,* edited by Imre Hamar and Takami Inoue, 7–14. Budapest: Institute for East Asian Studies, 2016.

Okazaki, Joji. *Pure Land Buddhist Painting.* Translated by Elizabeth ten Grotenhuis. Tokyo: Kodansha International, 1977.

Pannyanada, Sao. "Saddha (Faith) is the Fundamental Step to Become a Buddhist." Accessed January 12, 2016. http://www.myanmarnet.net/nibbana/article1.htm.

Pap, Melinda. "The Concept of Faith in Zhanran's Diamond Scalpel Treatise." In *Faith in Buddhism,* edited by Imre Hamar and Takami Inoue, 49–65. Budapest: Institute for East Asian Studies, 2016.

Park, Sung Bae. *Buddhist Faith and Sudden Enlightenment.* Albany: State University of New York Press, 1983.

Pauling, Chris. *Introducing Buddhism.* USA: Barnes & Noble, 1990.

Payne, Richard K. "Intertwined Sources of Modernistic Opposition to Ritual: History, Philosophy, Culture." *Religions* 9, no. 11 (2018) 366. https://doi.org/10.3390/rel9110366.

Porcu, Elisabetta. *Numen Book Series: Pure Land Buddhism in Modern Japanese Culture.* Leiden: Brill, 2008.

Port, Dosho. *Keep Me in Your Heart A While: The Haunting Zen of Dainin Katagiri.* Chicago: Wisdom, 2009.

The Pratyutpanna Samadhi Sutra and the Surangama Samadhi Sutra. Translated by Paul Harrison and John McRae. Berkeley: Numata Center for Buddhist Translation and Research, 1998.

Salzberg, Sharon. *Faith: Trusting Your Own Deepest Experience.* USA: Riverhead, 2003.

Sakurai, Shuyu. "Zenshū ni Okeru" 禅宗に於ける [In the Zen Sect]. Daihōrin 大法輪 45, no. 5 (1978) 138.

Sansom, George. *Japan: A Short Cultural History.* New York: Appleton-Century-Crofts, 1943.

Scheder, David Bowman. *Japanese Buddhism.* Japan: Yokohama Bunsha, 1899.

Scott, David. "Hindu and Christian Bhakti: A Common Human Response to the Sacred." *Indian Journal of Theology* 29, no. 1 (1980) 12–32.

Sekido, Norio. "Bhakti and Sraddha." *Journal of Indian and Buddhist Studies* 41, no. 1 (1992) 984–993.

Selkirk, Jean. "The Role of Devotion in Sewing Buddha's Robe." Ancient Way: A Journal of Traditional Soto Zen Practice (March 15, 2018). https://ancientwayjournal.wordpress.com/2018/03/15/the-role-of-devotion-in-sewing-buddhas-robe.

Sharf, Robert. *Coming to Terms with Chinese Buddhism: A Reading of the Treasure Store Treatise.* Honolulu: University of Hawai'i Press, 2002.

Sharf, Robert. "On Pure Land Buddhism and Ch'an/Pure Land Syncretism in Medieval China." *T'oung Pao* 88, no. 4 (2003) 282–331.

———. Sharf, Robert. *The Treasure Store Treatise (Pao-tsang lun) and the Sinification of Buddhism in Eighth-century China.* Michigan: University of Michigan Press, 1991.

———. Sharf, Robert. "Whose Zen? Zen Nationalism Revisited." In *Rude Awakenings: Zen, the Kyoto School, & the Question of Nationalism,* edited by James W. Heisig and John C. Maraldo. Honolulu: University of Hawai'i Press, 1995.

Sheng-Yen. *Attaining the Way: A Guide to the Practice of Chan Buddhism.* Boston: Shambhala, 2006.

Sheng-Yen. *Chan Practice and Faith.* Taiwan: Dharma Drum Mountain, 2009.

Shibayama, Zenkei. *A Flower Does Not Talk: Zen Essays.* Translated by Sumiko Kudo Tokyo: Charles. E. Tuttle, 1997.

Shigaraki, Takamaro. *Heart of the Shin Buddhist Path: A Life of Awakening.* Chicago: Wisdom Publications, 2013.

Soeng, Mu. *Trust in Mind: The Rebellion of Chinese Zen.* Boston: Wisdom, 2004.

Sugawara, Kenshu. "Kesa Kudoku: Virtue of the Kashaya." Accessed January 10, 2018. https://global.sotozen-net.or.jp/eng/library/key_terms/pdf/key_terms05.pdf.

Sugiyama, Shigeki. "The Essence of Shinran's Teaching." In *Engaged Pure Land Buddhism: The Challenges of Jodo-Shinshu in the Contemporary World*, edited by Tanaka, Kenneth and Eisho Nasu. Berkeley, CA: Wisdom Ocean, 1998.

Suzuki, Daisetsu Teitaro. *An Introduction to Zen Buddhism*, Evergreen Black Cat ed. New York: Grove, 1964.

Sweeping Zen. "Sei'un An Roselyn Stone Interview." Accessed February 15, 2015. http://sweepingzen?com/seiun-an-roselyn-stone-interview-2/.

Tam, Thich Thien. *Buddhism of Wisdom and Faith: Pure Land Principles and Practice*. California: International Buddhist Monastic Institute, 1991.

Tanaka, Kenneth K. "Where is the Pure Land?: Controversy in Chinese Buddhism on the Nature of Pure Land." *Pacific World Journal (New Series)* 3, (1987) 36–45.

Taves, Ann. "No Field Is an Island: Fostering Collaboration Between the Academic Study of Religion and the Sciences." *Method and Theory in the Study of Religion* 22, no. 2. (2010) 170–188.

Thera, Nanamoli. *Does Saddha Mean Faith?* Kandy: Buddhist Publication Society, 1963.

Thera, Nyanaponika. *Devotion in Buddhism: Three Essays*. Kandy: Buddhist Publication Society, 2008.

Thera, Soma. *Faith in the Buddha's Teachings and Refuge in the Triple Gem*. Kandy: Buddhist Publication Society, 2009.

Torei, Enji. *The Undying Lamp of Zen: The Testament of Zen Master Torei*. Translated by Thomas Cleary. London: Shambhala, 2010.

Tricycle.org. "Is Faith Important in Buddhism?" Accessed December 9, 2020. https://tricycle.org/beginners/buddhism/is-faith-important-in-buddhism/.

Tsong-Kha-Pa. *The Great Treatise on the Stages of the Path to Enlightenment*. Translated by Lamrim Chenmo Translation Committee, reprint ed. USA: Snow Lion, 2014.

Uchiyama, Kosho. *Opening the Hand of Thought: Foundations of Zen Buddhist Practice*. Chicago: Wisdom, 2004.

Vasubandhu. *Seven Works of Vasubandhu*. Translated by Stefan Anacker. Delhi: Motilal Banarsidass, 2008.

von Bruck, Michael and Whalen Lai. *Buddhismus und Christentum: Geschichte, Konfrontation, Dialogue*. Muchen: Beck, 2000.

Williams, Paul. *Mahayana Buddhism: The Doctrinal Foundations*. London: Routledge, 1989.

Yamada, Koun. *Zen: The Authentic Gateway*. USA: Wisdom, 2015.

Yamamoto, Kosho. *The Mahayana Mahaparinirvana Sutra in 12 Volumes*. Translated and edited by Tony Page. London: Nirvana Publications, 2000.

Yun, Hsing. *Being Good: Buddhist Ethics for Everyday Life*. Taiwan: Buddha's Light, 2009.

Zengaku Daijiten 禪學大辭典. [A Comprehensive Dictionary of The Zen Lineage]. Tōkyō: Taishūkan Shoten, 1985.

Zhang, Shenyan. *Minmatsu Chūgoku Bukkyō no Kenkyū: Tokuni Chigyoku o Chūshin to Shite* 明末中國佛教の研究:特に智旭を中心として [A Study of Chinese Buddhism: Focusing on Zhixu]. Tōkyō: Sankibō Busshorin, 1975.

Zhixu, Ouyi. *Mind Seal of the Buddha: Patriarch Ou-I's Commentary on the Amitabha Sutra*. Translated by Jonathon Christopher Cleary. New York: Sutra Translation Committee of the United States and Canada, 1997.

www.ingramcontent.com/pod-product-compliance
Lightning Source LLC
Chambersburg PA
CBHW070743030726
47601CB00001B/124